Aug. 29 - 1977

To
Mary Ann Sodlo
With thanks.
for an interesting
discussion

Blair Vaughn

TAPPING THE HUMAN RESOURCE
A STRATEGY FOR PRODUCTIVITY

TAPPING THE

HUMAN RESOURCE
A STRATEGY FOR PRODUCTIVITY

CLAIR F. VOUGH
WITH
BERNARD ASBELL

amacom
A DIVISION OF AMERICAN MANAGEMENT ASSOCIATIONS

To the innovative co-workers
with whom I have been associated
over the years

Library of Congress Cataloging in Publication Data
Vough, Clair F
   Tapping the human resource.

   Includes bibliographical references and index.
   1. Wages and labor productivity—Case studies.
2. International Business Machines Corporation.
Office Products Division. I. Asbell, Bernard, joint
author. II. Title.
HD4945.V68   658.3'14   74-23473
ISBN 0-8144-5370-8

FOREWORD

Clair Vough says we can improve productivity by utilizing people's minds as well as their hands. That, in a sentence, summarizes this book. But don't be misled by that sentence—or the book's title—into thinking this is just another theoretical discussion of productivity improvement or a humanistic appeal for "job enlargement" or "job enrichment." The book is not a soft-headed, bleeding-heart appeal for a human-relations utopia where everybody is happy and content, whistling at their work. Rather, it is concrete and practical.

Vough draws on ten years of direct experience in which he

increased productivity in the Office Products Division of IBM, which primarily manufactures electric typewriters. It's a tough business: The competition is fierce, and the manufacturing work is precision, repetitive, and nonglamorous. As in other businesses, the people are a mixture of skilled, semi-skilled, and unskilled workers and managers—with their assorted fears, suspicions, and hopes. What Vough has proved—and documented with detailed examples—is that tapping the human resource, in the particular way he did, led to increased productivity, human satisfaction, and profit.

Vough acknowledges that people often don't work up to their potential, that much work is boring and depersonalized, that job dissatisfaction is rampant. He argues that job enlargement and enrichment—which merely add variety or increased duties—will not result in real satisfaction or productivity. Only *responsibility* will: total responsibility in a vertically organized job with a person's name on it. Vough maintains that responsibility should be placed where the work is—and with the lowest-ranking person possible. Every person in a job knows that job best, so he or she is the person most likely to perceive new ways to make that job efficient. And any job can be made more efficient if the person doing it has responsibility, accountability, and motivation in the form of pay and promotion.

With that as his thesis, Vough shows in chapter after chapter how he improved productivity over ten years at a number of IBM plants, both inside and outside the United States. He spells out the policies that flow from this central theme: pay for productivity, promotion for productivity, full employment, work simplification, and others.

Several things are important about this book. First, it comes at a time when the world is in the grip of simultaneous inflation and recession, slowed economic growth, and food and energy shortages. People are increasingly questioning whether our economic machine can stand these strains. It is recognized that increased productivity may be the answer—

but national rates of productivity increases are declining. The more pessimistic among us are asking: Do people really want to produce and achieve more? And can growth ever be reconciled with human dignity and satisfaction in work?

Vough's answer is a clear and positive *yes*. Productivity can be increased, profits can be increased, and people can find pride, dignity, and motivation in their work. There is no magic to this. It goes back to the real source of power and achievement—the mind of the individual human being.

Second, this book comes at a time when we have been extracting very high productivity gains from the substitution of mechanical and electrical power for manual labor, particularly in the manufacturing and agricultural sectors. But the rapid gains from this substitution process are nearing their limits. And with the less productive services sector making up more and more of our GNP and labor force, we will have to secure larger productivity gains from all sectors, particularly from services. Peter Drucker has made the same point in his discussion of the new "knowledge society" in which the human being—his brain and his will, not his brawn—is the principal ingredient for improving productivity. Vough shows us how.

Third, Vough contradicts a lot of prevailing conventional wisdom about productivity improvement. Namely:

—that improved productivity means working harder and faster;

—that improved productivity comes about almost solely through capital investment and growth of the labor force;

—that improved productivity means cost-cutting, cutbacks, and unemployment;

—that improved productivity means reducing the quality of goods, the quality of work, and the quality of life.

Vough says not so, and he presents convincing arguments and case histories to show that none of these things have to result. Assuming that he is right (and I think he is), then we don't have to be pessimistic about our potential for greater productivity and the prospect of our losing the will to work in an increasingly depersonalized world.

I found Vough's thesis especially meaningful because it coincides with my own direct experience in two other environments: academic and governmental. In the university, I have seen similar responses—in both human satisfaction and increased productivity—when I placed responsibility and accountability at the lowest possible levels and rewarded people accordingly. As chairman of the Price Commission during Phase II of the Economic Stabilization Program, I found the same to be true in the governmental arena. I delegated important responsibilities to people at almost unheard-of lower civil service levels throughout the Price Commission. People who had never before felt such pride and involvement in the federal service became turned-on to their work, took tremendous pride in what they did, and produced results that astounded both them and the most critical observers. Like Vough, I used no special tricks—just responsibility, accountability, and rewards.

It is refreshing to see such a book published now, at a time when people hear so many gloomy ideas advanced about reduced productivity, job boredom, blue collar blues, alienation, limits to growth, and the like. It is refreshing because the book says we don't have to accept any of this as inevitable —that *we*, the human resource, are the answer to the problems we have created.

Vough has made a real contribution, not only by writing this book, but by actually doing things instead of just talking about them. As Dizzy Dean said, "It ain't braggin' if you done it." Vough has done it. You should read about it and then do something about it.

C. Jackson Grayson, Jr.
DEAN, SCHOOL OF BUSINESS ADMINISTRATION
SOUTHERN METHODIST UNIVERSITY

PREFACE

For more than forty years, I have been fortunate in working for a company whose policies have permitted me to grow from subassembler to division vice president. During this period, I observed and learned a great deal from the people with whom I worked and the managers for whom I worked.

When, in 1956, I was given overall responsibility for manufacturing in the Electric Typewriter (now the Office Products) Division, I drew heavily on my past observations and experiences. IBM's fundamental policies of respect for and fairness to every individual (as firmly laid down by Thomas

J. Watson, Sr., and reaffirmed by his successors) gave us the latitude and encouragement to develop the programs outlined in this book.

The success of these programs is due to the efforts of the creative and dedicated people in our Office Products plants in the United States, Europe, Canada, and Latin America. Space does not permit me to mention everyone who should be credited. However, the following people were in positions of leadership which set the tone of the plants: Ed Durbeck in Lexington, Kentucky; John Murphy in Lexington, Kentucky; Bob Stevens in IBM World Trade Corporation, Lexington, Kentucky; Charles Muller in Austin, Texas; Dick Deatrick in Boulder, Colorado; Jack Harris in Toronto, Canada; Herman Schwab in Berlin, Germany; Guenter Preiss in Berlin, Germany; Frans Kraak in Amsterdam, Holland; Gerrit (George) Prins in Amsterdam, Holland; Michel Laudier in Boigny, France; Tony Casella in Sumare, Brazil; Heinz Schwabe in Bogotá, Colombia; Tony Murua in Mexico City, Mexico; and Julio Renoud in Mexico City, Mexico.

Mike Flynn, Bill Ablin, and Harrell (Tex) Shaver of Lexington, Kentucky, made major contributions to the writing of this book. And the one who coordinated all our efforts during the writing of the manuscript was my assistant, Winona Rose, with help from Sue Reynolds.

Clair F. Vough

CONTENTS

INTRODUCTION

Over the past four decades, the International Business Machines Corporation has grown into one of the giants of the industrial world. Its people are known for their esprit de corps. Industrial managers, although sensing and even admiring this esprit, rarely emulate the policies that brought it about. Their most frequent explanation for not doing so is that IBM is a special kind of company with a special kind of product, needing a special kind of people; thus it treats people in a special way. After all, its chief business is computers, employing people of advanced education and technical training who are ambitious to get ahead in a growth industry. Therefore IBM's experience doesn't apply to industries that have fully matured, where competition is fierce, and where the work of manufacturing is workaday and repetitive—often conceived as mindless.

Well, there is nothing special about the part of the business I'm in. The people in my division of IBM make typewriters, dictating machines, copiers, and supplies for these machines—but mostly typewriters—in ten plants around the world. There's nothing glamorous about it. Making typewriters is no more sophisticated than the manufacture of any precision machine. It is a tough business. The typewriter is one of the few products that can enter the United States absolutely duty-free, so we're wide open to competition, both domestically and internationally.

Financially, Office Products is now as healthy as any division in the very healthy company of IBM. More than to any other single factor, this can be attributed to methods developed over a long period for giving every person in our division a tangible, visible, *personal* stake in the division's productivity.

Our methods are applicable to virtually all types of manufacturing companies. They also are applicable to many non-manufacturing companies and work groups. Recently I have been working with government officials who are apparently convinced that our methods are applicable to productivity in government, particularly to massive clerical tasks such as those performed by the Social Security Administration.

In the past few years I have found myself spending increasing amounts of time receiving groups of management colleagues from other industries at our main plant in Lexington, Kentucky, and giving talks to managers elsewhere, about the way we have done things in our Office Products plants. We show our visitors what we do, tell what we do, and explain why. The managers listen, ask questions, tour the plant and observe, nod approvingly, and say they get it. Yet most of the time they *don't* get it.

When they say they get it, I think what they're saying is that what we do seems logical. It *ought* to work. It's the way they would *like* companies and people to behave toward one another. So these visitors like what they see. But because most of us trust what is familiar and distrust what is different, I have come to believe that most of these visiting managers do not quite trust what they see. When they go back, most of them keep doing just what they did before they came.

Perhaps the story of what we have learned—the experience, sometimes painful, sometimes very satisfying, and the methods our experience has led to—can best be put across this way, in a book. Let's begin at the beginning.

In the mid-1950s, IBM came near to going out of the typewriter business, which it had entered in 1933. Our competitors, both foreign and domestic, had discovered the market for electrically driven typewriters and were giving us a hard time. Our machine was expensive to produce and the profit was not in it. In 1955, the company set us up as a separate division, on the theory that by operating separately we could shave costs. And we were given an ultimatum: Either make the typewriter profitable or the division would be sold. The new division was moved out of Poughkeepsie into its own quarters *1956-7* at Kingston, New York. A year later, when our main plant was built in Lexington, the division moved into it.

Most of what I describe in this story has to do with the period from 1955 through 1966 and our oldest (for years our only) product, the typebar typewriter. This is the familiar machine that has a bar for each letter snapping up to imprint a sheet of paper sliding by in a carriage. Over the years, we have developed other major products—the dictating machine, the Copier, and the Selectric typewriter. In the Selectric, the letters are clustered on a single plated plastic ball which moves along the sheet of paper—no typebars, no moving carriage. Although the experiences told here are drawn mostly from the history of the typebar machine, let me emphasize that the same management methods governed all production in our plants, new products as well as old, and the results were fully as rewarding.

This book deals mainly with how we increased productivity in manufacturing the typebar typewriter. "Productivity" is now a magical catchword of industry. To me, it is not a catchword, but hard arithmetic. It is the ratio of output (in goods or services) to dollar input (both direct and indirect). When output per dollar spent is increased, productivity is improved. Improved productivity, which may mean improvement of profit and employee benefits, may also mean more dollars available for expansion, product improvement, new product development, new investment, sales promotion, strengthened competitive position, and ultimately the creation of more jobs and an expanded economy. Improved productivity is the most important and constant challenge to business.

Productivity ought to be discussed in arithmetic terms, in manhours and dollars and cents. In discussing the productivity of the typebar typewriter, for the most part I will have to describe the improvement in terms of fractions or percentages, not manhours or dollars and cents, for reasons of company confidentiality that any manager in a competitive industry will appreciate. The significant points of this story will not suffer by this limitation.

When the electric typewriter was divisionalized in 1955, production of a single machine consumed x manhours of labor (which equaled a substantial portion of a 40-hour week). In our few months at Kingston, immediately after divisionalizing, we reduced that time by a couple of hours. In 1956, when we moved to Lexington, we really went to work on the problem. To sum up the story fast, by 1966 we had slashed x by 65 percent.

During that period, of course, the cost of an hour of labor rose sharply. One might ask, then, whether our improvement in hourly productivity was paralleled by a reduction of cost.

We are now paying over 100 percent more per hour than we paid in 1955. Yet our typewriter today, in 1974, costs less to produce than it did when our productivity campaign began.

The flat statement can be made that if we were still putting x hours into the manufacture of a typewriter, there would be no Office Products Division of IBM today—at least, it would not be making electric typewriters.

The next thing one might ask is, "What happened to quality?" In the beginning we measured ourselves by what we called "out-of-box" quality—the number of machines requiring service at the time the customers took them out of the box. We agreed on setting a goal of no more than 25 percent of machines requiring out-of-box service. Well, that figure soon dipped below 10 percent. We either had to be satisfied with that low figure or find some new measurement to give us a more significant challenge. In 1960 we changed the criterion of quality measurement to "warranty time." How much *time* did an IBM Customer Engineer have to spend servicing a machine (including special problems of installation) in the first 90 days of its use? When we started out with this much tougher criterion, we averaged a certain fraction of an hour per machine over a three-month period. Five years later, we had cut that warranty service time exactly in half, and have since reduced it further. Clearly, the people back at the plant were doing their work not only faster but better.

There is more to these productivity achievements than hits the naked eye. Between 1955 and 1966, besides taking two-thirds of the time out of manufacturing the typewriter, besides cutting costs by 45 percent (at higher pay scales), and besides cutting warranty service time drastically, we saved an enormous amount by avoiding unnecessary plant construction and purchases of manufacturing equipment. If we were putting out today's production at our old productivity rate of 1955, our present plant would require an additional 1 million square feet of floor space, plus the expensive machinery

¼ capital substd labor
¼ engineering
½ people output
savings.

to fill it—just for typewriters. Even more significant, the improved productivity has financially permitted us to build a first-rate staff of development engineers, leading to the design and introduction of the Selectric, the Copier, and other new office products, and the building of new plants in Austin, Texas, and in countries overseas.

The time came when we wanted to make sure that we at Lexington fully understood how that achievement had come about. Just what was responsible for cutting those hours out of typewriter manufacture? Analyzing it closely, we found that a quarter of the saving could be attributed to increased mechanization of production. Another quarter was due to engineering changes in the typewriter itself. Fully half of the saving came directly from increased output by *people*—human work. People were working more intelligently, more productively, and more accurately. Every measure we had, including quarterly attitude surveys, showed that most of our people were relatively happy in their jobs, felt involved in trying to increase productivity, and felt rewarded for their gains. Our labor turnover stood roughly at 2 percent, about one-third the usual rate for comparable manufacturing industries.

When thinking about productivity, many managers start by considering how to cut costs—how to reduce the total production budget. Most often, they start with ways to reduce the payroll. From both a business and humanitarian point of view, in my opinion, that is almost always wrong. When we started out to improve our productivity—battling for our life as an IBM division—instead of going to work on reduction of expenses, we went to work on increasing production. If we could get more typewriters going out the back door, divided into the same expense package that we started with, we'd achieve the same goal. Nobody's morale—nobody's desire to produce more—has ever been raised by a campaign to cut expenses, especially when it's by some arbitrary amount.

The basic tenet of traditional industrial engineering is that a factory worker can be manipulated, through time and motion study procedures and other techniques, into enriching his company at the expense of himself. The truth is that the man on the job can outfox the company almost every time. Nobody is going to work faster or better if it means cutting his own throat, especially if working faster or better may eliminate his job or the job of a co-worker. I learned this during my own 14 years on the assembly line. In the mid-1930s, a line of us were working on tabulating machines that had been rede-signed to be more trouble-free in the assembly stage. Word got out that our project manager planned to take one of the two inspectors off the job. The new ''trouble-free'' machines soon developed every imaginable kind of trouble until ma-chines were backed up half the length of the room. Instead of taking one inspector off, the manager had to add one. So we now had three men instead of two—doing one man's work. This continued until the machine was obsoleted.

People—and their brains—are the most precious resource we have in our shop. We want to improve our productivity not at the expense of our people, but at the expense of wasted time, lost motion, unnecessary bureaucracy, and red tape. Our most valuable partners in cutting waste are the people on the production floor, who know their jobs better than anyone. We want the involvement of their minds as well as their hands—and we pay them for it. A sound system for increasing pro-ductivity should reward the people on the production line as well as the company. It should never threaten the pay enve-lope, the job security, or the opportunities for advancement of people who become more productive.

Nobody in this world works at top capacity. I saw a survey once that said the average person works at about 30 percent of his capacity.* I don't know how that figure was arrived at, but I won't quarrel with it. The point is that everyone has a

---

* The pronouns ''he,'' ''his,'' and ''him'' in this book are used for the sake of grammatical simplicity; they are not intended to exclude women. Of course, many production-line workers and an increasing number of managers are female.

great deal of untapped, reserve capability. If a person perceives that working harder is a threat to him, he will work less—leave more of his capability in reserve. On the other hand, if that person perceives that working harder and better will fatten his pay envelope and increase his chances of getting ahead, he will work more effectively—draw more from his untapped reserve. This is not theory, at least not to us. It has been a reality, and a reality that has profited both the company and its people. It was the foundation of our policy.

While that underlying principle is stated simply, the practices that flow from it are complex and have fingered their way through everything we did. The policy was total, pervasive, and consistent. Without that totality and consistency, it would not be a policy at all and would not work.

What are those practices? The following paragraphs are not only a brief summary of them, but are indeed a road map of where this book will take us, chapter by chapter:

Pay. Each person's pay should be determined by his or her contribution to the business. In our plants, merit pay increases were earned solely on productivity—not on previous education or experience, or "attitude," or any other intangible that did not result directly in increased contribution. When this pay-for-production policy is stated simply, it often gets the response, "Oh, you mean you paid by piece rate." Not at all. Piece-rate pay is an anti-incentive for increased productivity. Our policy provided a true incentive, as Chapter 1 will show.

Promotion. Like pay increases, promotions were given solely on work contribution. When a vacancy occurred, candidates to fill it were considered only from among the top producers in the next lower grade level—whether or not the work performed in the next lower level was related to the work required in the vacant job. We went on the theory (no, not the theory, the successful practice) that if a job opens up for, say, a toolmaker, and if a top-producing machine operator wants that job, he should be a top candidate for it. Even

union?
attitude

though we have to train him for the new job, our experience has shown that he is more likely to become a more efficient toolmaker than many present toolroom operators who are not as highly motivated. Even for promotions into and up through management, objective measures of work contribution were our chief guide.

Full employment. People crave to be more productive, provided that increased productivity does not threaten their jobs. Merit pay and merit promotion reward people for working faster and better, but those policies can work only if people feel absolutely secure that they are not speeding themselves (or anyone else) into unemployment. Therefore, to enlist its people's cooperation in increasing productivity, a company must do everything possible to insure the steady employment of every competent employee. Management has the responsibility to plan production so as to generate year-round work for all its people through what we call "buffering," which I'll describe in Chapter 2. We have pursued a practice of full employment through bad years as well as good, including the worst days of the Great Depression—and it has paid off in loyalty and productivity.

Work simplification. The genius required for figuring out how to do more work with less effort lies with the people who do the job. We teach *all* of our people—from top to bottom—the "secrets" that industrial engineers use for analyzing motion, efficiency, and so on. Secure that he will not lose his job by eliminating work, each person becomes his own efficiency expert. We reward the good use of his mind, as well as his hands, with pay raises and promotion. The results have been spectacular.

Workmanship analysis. The success of our company is founded on high quality, which we have no intention of compromising. Every IBM employee must be committed to it. Having transplanted to our factory a university course in *efficiency*, we set about to find a course in quality *craftsmanship* that we could also transplant. We found none anywhere in the United States. So we created our own, giving it to every employee, top to bottom—again, with superb results.

Total responsibility. This is at the heart of our policy. A person cares more about his work when he—and everyone else—knows it is his. The old industrial theory has been that the more you can reduce a task into specialized jobs, the more efficient the production line. We are reversing that. We are shortening our production lines drastically and are making each person responsible for discrete, expanded responsibilities so he can say, "This part of the typewriter is mine." Our goal is to eliminate inspectors, both in-line and end-of-line.

Vertical management. As with production-line people, the quantity and quality of work produced under a manager should be traceable directly to him. Management should be designed vertically to encompass specific products and services wherever possible, not horizontally by function.

Goals. Every project and department should have an annual goal, attainable by stretching. As many as possible of the people involved in achieving the goal should also be involved in setting it. Attainment of the goal should produce a benefit—not a threat—to those who achieve it.

Simplified business. Productivity gains made on the production line are too often lost through expensive waste in the front office. Often, inventory control on small, inexpensive parts costs more than the parts themselves. In our movement toward total responsibility, we are experimenting with assigning much of our inventory control, even purchasing functions, to the production-line people who use the parts. We are examining every paper-pushing function to see if it carries its productivity weight. We are moving in on "cost generators," expensive and unnecessary functions that breed further costs to justify their existence. Our goal is more typewriters and less paper.

Departmental workshops. This is our newest and potentially most productive program for encouraging people to use their minds as well as their hands. Executives and engineers have long valued the creative tool of brainstorming, but who has ever called meetings of assemblers, machinists, and stockroom clerks to brainstorm under the leadership of their department manager? We have! And with remarkable results. They have identified production problems that remote "experts" might never have perceived, and have devised imaginative, cost-saving solutions. Most important, this form of creativity provides a big lift to morale through a sense of company participation.

The manager. A manager must feel in his bones the policies he is charged with executing. He must be attuned to *people* at least as much as to policies and production goals. He must symbolize company policy, fostering confidence not only in him but in the policy itself, helping advance productivity as everybody's common goal.

Innovators and innovation. A creative idea may produce more cost reduction—and more production—than a roomful of experts. Great ideas sometimes come in peculiar ways: They often come from the most unexpected sources, sometimes masquerading as a gripe. The care and cultivation of innovators and innovation is an art that every manager should master.

Improving the status and recognition of manufacturing people. Most companies have dinners and prizes for salesmen who do good work—knowing the tribute will spur them on—but seldom do we honor the man or woman who is outstanding in producing the goods. Production people are as human as salespeople. They, too, are spurred by recognition and pride. We have instilled dedication and pride in our production managers and work constantly to foster similar pride on the production lines.

1

PAY FOR PRODUCTIVITY— ONLY FOR PRODUCTIVITY

The most crucial single thing that motivates people to greater productivity is a three-letter word—*pay*.

Not many people agree with me. Obviously, not many employers do, when you consider how much creative effort they put into the illusion that they are adding a thin layer to their profits by shaving that layer from wages. Nor do many of the "experts"—social scientists who take surveys and write articles—agree with me. In survey after survey, they conclude that the biggest motivators are less tangible than pay: such things as "job satisfaction," "social status," and varieties thereof that elude specific definition. In most of these surveys, pay ranks somewhere around sixth. For all their hair-splitting research, my experience tells me that they're wrong.

Certainly, status and job satisfaction are important, and they are vital concerns of our productivity policy. But go down the list of the status-and-satisfaction factors at your company, and for each factor ask yourself what would happen if it were removed. You'd still have a labor force showing up for work come Monday morning. Perhaps a very effective labor force. But cut a man's pay below what he thinks he can earn down the street—and then see how long he stays around.

Furthermore, pay is a source of pride, security, and satisfaction for the entire family. Thus, good pay enlists the support of important allies—a reward at home as well as at the pay window. Don't sell that short.

This is scarcely any private discovery of mine. The old-fashioned idea that pay is a prime motivator has always been an underlying principle of IBM policy: Offer more pay than competing employers and get the best people available. This has been not an expensive policy but a profitable one.

My purpose is not to pit pay *against* other motivators, particularly the motivator of opportunity for advancement (a form of status). They are, in fact, inseparable. I will examine them separately, however, for the purposes of detailed study. In this chapter, I will emphasize our unique system of merit pay and in the next, merit promotion. The word "merit," and exactly what we mean by it, is the crux of both chapters. Our goal is increased productivity. The merit that interests us is work that helps achieve that goal.

Salary ranges for various levels of skill or responsibility, which are constantly reviewed in accordance with changing national averages and trends, are set by IBM corporate headquarters. In Office Products manufacturing during the period covered by this book, an individual's pay within the salary range of his job was determined only by his productivity.

Only is an absolute, and I mean it absolutely. It took us

years to refine pay for productivity down to an absolute, and we believe we've got the impurities pretty well out of it.

Early in the game, we had decided that the only two things that should affect a person's pay were *production* and *quality*. We soon realized that that wasn't pure enough. A manager still had to weigh a producer's quality against his productivity, a clear invitation to letting the manager's personal judgment intrude. If someone produces high quantity, but at the cost of consistent high quality, how much do you "demerit" his productivity achievement?

This brought up a more critical question: Could we tolerate below-par quality? Certainly not. In a business like ours, inferior quality is unacceptable. That's all there is to it. High quality cannot be a factor in a person's pay rate, but a *condition of his employment*. If someone can't meet the quality standards of one job, we'll try him on two or three others. Very rarely do we fail to find a job he can do well. In that extremely rare case, we just have to let that person go.

Having made quality a requirement and not a comparative measure of merit, we were down to the simple, hard core of our policy. We pay for productivity. *Only* productivity.

How does our policy of pay for productivity work? What are its mechanics?

Like most organizations, we classify jobs into various levels of skill or responsibility, each level with its own pay range. Many plants call these "wage levels." At IBM everyone is on a weekly salary rather than an hourly wage, so we go by the term "salary levels." (A salary system, rather than an hourly wage system, is essential to our merit pay and merit promotion policy for reasons that will soon be clear.) In our plant, almost all jobs below the managerial level are in Level 20 and below—starting at Level 11. (I don't know what ever happened to Levels 1 through 10.)

But that does not mean each skill level has a single rate of pay. Within each level a person may rise through four pay quartiles. Pay raises within a salary level are based purely on productivity—the number of pieces a person turns out.

(Similarly, promotion to the next salary level is based purely on productivity, but that gets us ahead of our story.)

Let's visualize this through a simple, fictional example. Sam Johnson's job is to attach five parts to a carriage assembly. We'll call his skill level—or salary level—X. Let's say a good producer in that job, according to our long-term experience, can handle 320 carriage assemblies a week. When Sam begins that job—and his production is lower because he's just learning it—he may do 290 pieces a week. His salary level for that production rate (and I remind you that these figures are hypothetical) is $145. Soon his production increases to 320 pieces per week. That puts Sam into the next higher pay quartile within his salary level, say, $160 a week. Through increased manual skill, and perhaps a good time-saving idea that makes his work more efficient, Sam then moves up to 350 pieces a week, an outstanding production rate. This pushes him up into the highest of the four pay quartiles in his salary level—let's say, $175 a week. All these pay raises are *within* the range of his salary level, X.

The raises are earned automatically and objectively—based purely on productivity. No personal judgment by his manager. No guesswork. Sam need not lie awake in the middle of the night fretting, "Does my boss like me? Will he give me a raise?" If our policy is working correctly, Sam Johnson knows exactly where he stands—and so do we. He knows exactly what will entitle him to earn more money—and so do we.

Thus, of several employees in a given job, the one who consistently averages the highest production will receive the highest salary, and the least productive will receive the lowest salary. He knows why, and we know why. Note that term "consistently averages." A person cannot raise his pay by being a flash-in-the-pan producer for a week or two. Neither is his salary level endangered by a temporary setback resulting from illness, a temporarily poor state of mind, or some factor totally beyond his control, such as a run of defective parts, an inventory shortage, or a machine breakdown. We are interested in measuring *consistent* production over the longer range.

That is why a salary, rather than an hourly wage, is most compatible with our merit pay policy. Once a man or woman increases his or her skill in a job, that increased skill is reflected in a higher salary. This is the philosophic opposite of a piecework rate, by which a producer's income fluctuates from one hour to the next, depending upon pieces turned out. A piecework rate guarantees insecurity, therefore guaranteeing resentment. Our merit salary system assures a producer of salary security at a productivity level he has shown he can sustain—and promises a higher salary if his productivity increases.

Perhaps I should interject here that Sam Johnson, at salary level X, need not rise through all four pay quartiles of his salary level before being promoted to salary level Y. It may well be that while Sam is still in the third pay quartile of level X, a vacancy occurs in level Y—and his manager's records show that Sam is the top producer among all the people in level X. The promotion goes to Sam. Now suppose Sam had just achieved the top pay rate of level X before his promotion. It may happen—and often does—that the lowest pay rate in level Y is slightly below what Sam is already earning as a top producer in level X. Of course, his salary does not go down. In fact, he enters level Y at an increase over his present salary, with the added opportunity of rising through the pay quartiles of level Y.

How do we determine a proper production level for each pay rate—what a person "ought" to produce to earn a raise? Most plants resolve that question through a cold war between a time-study engineer and the people on the assembly line. The engineer develops a "scientific" notion of how long a particular job ought to take either through theoretical time-and-motion studies or through actual time studies of the job. The minute an assembler and his co-workers spy that engineer and his clipboard, they sense a self-interest in slowing down the work lest they get trapped into higher production for the same old hourly wage. Or, if theoretical studies are used, they resist the theoretical rates. Production goes up only at the expense of morale.

We, too, make theoretical cost estimates when a new procedure is being created in machining, assembling, finishing, and so forth. But these are *temporary* estimates, useful for 12 weeks or so, until we accumulate actual experience averages. We then modify or correct these estimates, based on actual experience, to arrive at expected production rates (EPRs).

Not every producer hits that expected production rate on the nose. We are wholly satisfied with a person who comes near a performance level of 95 percent. We are minimally satisfied with a person whose performance is below 90 percent but above 80 percent. A producer who does not rise beyond 80 percent after a reasonable period of training does not belong in that job. In happy contrast, a producer whose performance is between 100 and 110 percent is very likely his department's top producer. Performance above 110 percent is seldom achieved—not because the requirement is superhuman, but because so ambitious a producer will have already earned a promotion to the next salary level as soon as a vacancy can be found.

Those percentage categories are, in fact, rough definitions of the four pay quartiles within each salary level. They are listed in Table 1:

Table 1

PAY QUARTILE	PERFORMANCE PERCENT	INTERPRETIVE APPRAISAL RATING FOR WORK WHERE THERE IS NO NUMERICAL GUIDE
1	110–120	This range is seldom achieved.
2	100–110	This range is above that of most.
3	90–100	This is the wholly satisfactory range.
4	80–90	This is the minimum satisfactory range.
	Below 80	Unacceptable.

There may appear to be a contradiction here. If expected performance is frozen into a production rate, based on what a department has achieved in previous weeks, how can we expect to raise a department's productivity above a certain level?

The answer is that our estimated production rate *never* stands still. As methods, tools, or designs are changed, the rate is remeasured and changed—usually upward. Does that mean that we expect people to work harder and harder toward infinity, until they finally drop from exhaustion? Certainly not. The essence of our productivity drive is contained in a slogan: *Work Smarter, Not Harder.*

Our greatest productivity gains have been achieved not by doing more work, but by eliminating unnecessary work. Our productivity has been increased far more by good use of *minds* than by speedup of *hands.* We have trained Sam Johnson to be his own methods engineer. Through increases in pay, we stand constantly ready to reward him for making his own job more efficient—by use of his mind. A new, higher rate of pay is a new base for further increases. In each new assignment at each new skill level, he has an incentive to use his mind to find more efficient ways of doing the new job.

I recall one man, a pre-adjuster performing in the middle range for his skill, who got ahead by using his head. Among his tools—an air gun, a torque gun, screwdrivers—he had a bothersome spring hook. One day he complained to his manager, "I'm always getting that damn thing lost under a typewriter or behind those guns. Could you fix me up with a leather pouch to wear so I can stick that spring hook in it?" His manager happily accommodated him—and the man's production rate went up. Working harder? No, he just wasn't getting furious any more. An interesting sidelight: Three other people were doing similar work. Two of them adopted the leather pouch. All three pouch users have earned promotions; the inventor of the pouch has been promoted farthest, to a managerial level in engineering. (We've found that a person who devises a new method generally uses it best—and is most likely to devise other new methods that get him further ahead.) The fourth person, who didn't want to bother with the leather pouch, has moved up only one salary level in 12 years. He is an acceptable producer, but is satisfied to stay where he is.

This efficiency system—working smarter, not harder—will be discussed in more detail in Chapters 4 and 5, which deal with work simplification. Suffice it to say that as long as the good minds of ambitious producers are at work, and as long as they are rewarded fairly for their discoveries, the expected production rate can—and *does*—keep rising, without straining the physical effort of the producers.

So we are describing a system in which an expected production rate is monitored and reevaluated and, equally important, in which each individual producer must feel secure that he gets credit for his work. This system requires diligent record keeping by first-line (departmental) managers. If he keeps his records correctly, a manager has no problem determining everyone's relative contribution and awarding pay raises—which he should have full authority to award. To perform this essential record keeping, the manager maintains three main documents:

1. *Weekly departmental performance report.* Besides calculating the department's performance for a week and comparing it against that of the previous week, this report chronicles changes in the productivity of each department member. If someone's production has significantly slipped for several weeks, the change is a signal to the manager to go to that person and find out what is wrong. It may be a personal problem that the manager can help solve. It may be a procedural or technical problem beyond the producer's control, which the manager *must* solve.

2. *Quarterly history report.* This report, to be distributed to all production and engineering areas, covers every part and operation within the department, listing for each: (1) quan-

tity produced, (2) actual hours, (3) planned hours, (4) estimated time per 100 pieces, (5) actual pieces per hour, (6) planned pieces per hour. The report does not include setup, re-setup, or temporary operation; it is a _production_ report.

3. In addition to these departmental reports, the department manager maintains a _productivity chart_ for each employee. It is a running, annotated record of an employee's productivity for a 25-week period, showing the employee's production (taken from the record in the weekly performance chart) compared against the estimated production rate. A red line shows the employee's performance over the 25-week period, and an orange line shows expected performance over the same period. The chart also includes explanatory notes, such as illness of employee or a procedural breakdown affecting his production.

These are the tools that enable our policy of pay for productivity to operate objectively and automatically. They are also the tools for removing the most dangerous threat to our system. That threat is _favoritism_. Favoritism is what is most despised by every working person I have ever known. It ought to be equally despised by every manager, right up to the top, for it is the source of most industrial management problems. Let's examine this business of favoritism.

Look at any conventional appraisal sheet that helps a manager or personnel department determine whether someone "merits" a raise, and you find anywhere from 10 to 30 items. Few of them have the slightest thing to do with productivity. You find such items as "time at present task," "time since last raise," "attitude," "versatility," "flexibility," "ability to learn," "willingness to follow directions," and "initiative." All of these are demands for somebody's subjective judgment. Someone who rates highest on these items may plod along as the department's slowest producer, and vice versa. I've never known anyone in my life who, after seeing a conventional appraisal of himself, had any idea where he stood with regard to prospects for a pay raise and promotion.

Can one measure productivity in teaching objectively?

Everyone in a department knows who the top producers really are, and respects them for it. Resentment spreads like a poison when second-rate producers get salary increases because of the irrelevant ratings of an appraisal sheet. Employees consider the standard appraisal a tally sheet for favoritism.

The only way to combat favoritism is by a simple, clear, objective policy understood by all. Any exception to that policy will be considered favoritism—and probably *is* just that. If the policy is not hard and fast, it is not a policy at all. Production people will be dissatisfied, and their manager will lose their respect. The employees become disgruntled and the plant a less productive place.

In my early years as an assembler, when IBM was young and less experienced, I observed firsthand how favoritism works. What I observed then may still be seen in some companies today. There were two or three individuals who, after a day's work, would take their department manager to a barroom and take turns buying him beers. We didn't have a clear pay-raise system then. We all got raises, all right, but those three fellows were always a little ahead of everyone else—not in their work, but in their raises. Everybody knew it. Any manager who thinks wages in his department are a secret is extremely naive. Everyone knows what everybody else gets. Well, that was during the Depression when we were all glad just to have a job. But we knew the politics, we all resented those three men, and most of all we resented that manager.

Any appearance of favoritism is dangerous, even if it's only *appearance*. Just four or five years ago in Lexington— where I like to feel that our pay-for-productivity policy has thrown favoritism out the window—I got a call from a fellow in one of our manufacturing departments. (At IBM we have what we call an open-door policy. Any employee may ask to see any manager at any level, right up to the Chairman of the Board, if he feels he has a grievance that has been unsatisfied at a lower level.) Not one, but four people from this department came to see me, obviously agitated. "What does a guy have to do around here," their spokesman said, "to be upgraded?" It turned out that their manager had given someone a promotion within the department. I asked, Was he a top producer? The answer, with much hemming and hawing, amounted to "Yes, but——."

I checked the man's production record. He *was* the department's top producer, and by our objective standard was most deserving of the promotion. Then what was bothering the men?

What finally came out was that a few months earlier the top producer had arranged for the manager to buy an air conditioner at wholesale for his home. Knowing this, his co-workers waited for something nice to happen to him—some quid pro quo. And sure enough, soon came the promotion. The fact that he deserved it on merit was beclouded by the *appearance* of favoritism. What was really beclouded was the firmness of our policy. Everyone was hurt.

I took that incident as a failure of management. First, we had not put across our policy strongly and clearly enough so that everyone fully trusted it. Secondly, we had not fully educated our managers—at least, not this particular manager —as to the absolute necessity of avoiding any appearance of favoritism. A policy not only must be firm, simple, and clearly understood, but it must be trusted.

When we first put in this pay-for-productivity system, it frightened some of our managers who had been trained in older methods. These managers had trouble overlooking the irrelevancies of how people dress, comb their hair, use language—the supposed symbols of ambition and competence ingrained in them by all those appraisal sheets they used to fill out. Many doubted that this straightforward incentive system, aided by straightforward record keeping, would really pay off in increased productivity. They didn't believe it would work —until they saw it work. Perhaps most touchy of all, some of them feared (correctly) that our simple system would reduce their prerogative as managers to move some employees ahead while barring others.

When someone's chart shows he has earned a raise, his first-line manager not only is authorized to give it but *must* give it. Otherwise, he has—we all have—the problem of a disgruntled employee rightly knocking on the door of the plant manager's office; more important than that, our policy is threatened by everyone else's potential loss of trust in it. When I was plant manager, I'd go to the first-line manager and ask, "Why didn't that fellow get his raise?" Sometimes I got the answer: "I couldn't do anything about it because I'd already used up my wage budget." I would not accept that—and still don't. A policy is more important than a budget. I'd tell him to break the budget but to notify everyone concerned that he's doing so.

In the main, these managers soon realized that our simple system solved their most serious problems—or avoided them altogether. For example, when someone comes in asking about a raise, the manager need only reply, "Well, let's get the record out." If an error has been made, it's corrected right then and there. While we do not claim that we in our shop have solved all problems of discrimination against women and minority groups, we know that a person's sex or race cannot be used to bar that person's upward climb through the pay scale—not if his or her manager is keeping the records correctly. The only color that counts is on that upward line of the productivity graph.

Production people themselves were sometimes suspicious, too. They'd been hoodwinked before on previous jobs, working hard to get ahead and then seeing someone else promoted. As years went by, however, our quarterly attitude surveys showed a disappearance of these suspicions. People still have gripes, Lord knows—but not against our merit system. They gripe at perceived human failures in the system, when they feel it has been polluted by traces of favoritism.

There is no question that in our merit system pressure is

put on people. But they put it on themselves, willingly. They have the option of not putting themselves under pressure. Any person choosing not to compete to become a top producer knows that he need only continue doing satisfactory work and his job is secure. We have hundreds of satisfactory employees who appear perfectly content with a fair day's pay for a fair day's work—and we make sure they get that fair day's pay. But those who really want to earn their way up—and I mean *earn* their way up—have a right to expect that opportunity.

PROMOTION
FOR PRODUCTIVITY—
ONLY FOR PRODUCTIVITY

Having discussed the relatively simple (but apparently radical) policy of pay for productivity, we now turn to the less simple policy of promotion for productivity. I remind the reader again that these two subjects are separated for purposes of clear and detailed discussion. But they are inseparable parts of a *single* policy.

The way to get promoted at IBM Lexington—the *only* way —was to be the top producer in your department. The same charts and graphs that told a manager who was entitled to a raise in pay also identified who the top producers were. These people were automatically eligible for vacancies in the next higher salary level. *Automatically.*

I wish I could say that a top producer's eligibility for promotion was every bit as objective as eligibility for a pay increment within a salary level. Sometimes matters of judgment *subjective* did enter, particularly if the top producer's next promotion would be into management, or if a vacancy occurred and several eligible top producers in different departments or work functions were being considered for the job. But in all cases we tried to make the promotion decision on the basis of objective performance data, relying as little as possible on subjective opinion.

Before going into the details of how promotion for productivity works, it's important to identify certain age-old industrial practices that we want to avoid—practices we consider the enemy of productivity. *Practices to Avoid*

Chief among these is the old standard of *input of time* as a qualification for promotion. That standard (which is used in the teaching profession and the civil service as well as in business) is harmful to both the individual and the company. Measurements of time put in are destroyers of incentive.

Sometimes the standard is applied to time in training rather than time on the job. Recently I read a long, sad newspaper story about how craftsmanship is going to the dogs. It quoted a plumbing contractor in Lexington, Massachusetts, who complained: "I hired a young mechanic, sixteen years old. At first, he was very ambitious. He really wanted to qualify for his plumber's license. But after four years, when he got his license, he got slower and slower. I reminded him that *licenses* don't do the work. *Men* do."

Credentials mislead us constantly. A job opens somewhere for a welder, and it's given to a man who completed a two-year course in welding because it's assumed he must be twice as good as other applicants who completed only a one-year course. Still another person is turned down cold because he taught himself to weld in his own garage. Does the employer really know who is the best welder among them? More important, does he know anything about who among them has the greatest capacity for growth? My belief: The only fair way to judge a welder's future potential is by looking at the record of his past performance. Moreover, the personal qualities that motivated a person to become the best welder can motivate that person to other outstanding accomplishments. What gets our welding done? Course-completion certificates, or ambitious people of demonstrated top performance?

Perhaps the traditional system of apprenticeship offers us the clearest demonstration of our past errors. Like most corporations, IBM used to require that all toolroom apprentices, having begun at a standard wage, receive a prescribed wage increase after a prescribed number of hours of on-the-job training; another fixed increase after another fixed number of job hours; and so on. Progress and pay were determined entirely by time put in—not by what a person could actually put out. That all-too-common system, in which the laggards are treated the same way as high achievers, is neat, orderly, and easy to administer—but it is preposterous. It teaches the laggard that he'll do all right no matter what, and teaches the high achiever that there's no percentage in trying to do his best.

We decided we'd like to throw that system out. We wanted to quit frustrating good producers and rewarding poor ones. Soon after we were divisionalized—before our pay and promotion policies were fully developed—we in Office Products asked IBM corporate headquarters for permission to try an experiment: raising the pay of our toolroom apprentices according to production. *Only* production. No more automatic raises for *hours* of apprenticeship, but an automatic raise when an apprentice demonstrated—through actual units of good-quality production on the job—that he was becoming a toolmaker. We got the permission, and have been extremely satisfied with the results.

We tried another experiment. One of the most difficult and

precise jobs in our plant is that of the final aligning and adjusting of the typebar typewriter. Customer satisfaction largely depends on the perfection of this critical task. Good aligners and adjusters were always in short supply, partly because it took three to four years to train an aligner and adjuster. This shortage often created a bottleneck on the assembly line.

We told our candidates for aligning and adjusting: "We'll promote you into this advanced job and raise your pay just as fast as you learn it and improve your productivity." The result? A three-year training program for aligners and adjusters was reduced to about six months for most people. It was reduced not by us, but by the trainees. And our supply of skilled aligners and adjusters has ceased being a problem.

In the preceding chapter I observed that in any department it can be assumed that everyone knows how much everyone else is paid. The same can be said for the rank order of top producers. Everybody knows who they are. When a manager's records are at variance with this peer knowledge—which rarely happens—the manager had better be prepared to defend the accuracy of his records.

But still there are problems in determining who ought to get the next promotion. For example, we have a group of about 150 people who work on subassemblies. Their jobs, in the main, are graded at Levels 12 to 14, some people putting together a power frame, some a carriage assembly, some a cam-bearing support assembly, and so forth. To those subassembly people, who are relatively new in the business, promotions are extremely important. In these early levels, people learn to either trust or distrust the fairness of our promotion policy. Among, say, four power-frame assemblers, it's easy to identify the top producer. You just need to keep counting pieces. But when a vacancy occurs in Level 13, how do you determine the top producer among all those who do *different* jobs in Level 12? How do you choose between your top power-frame assembler and your top carriage assembler?

The best method we have so far devised is by a person's *production as a percentage of the expected production rate (EPR) for his product.* Thus if a power-frame assembler is hitting 108 percent of the EPR for power frames, he'll be promoted in preference to a carriage assembler hitting 103 percent for carriages. EPRs are issued by the estimating department and are revised in accordance with actual production experience.

If the percentage difference between them appears "too close to call," the managers of the various subassembly units will take into account other objective factors, such as the previous production histories of the candidates. The candidate who just misses out on a promotion this time is assured by his manager that he's still in line for another vacancy. It has been our consistent experience that people are understanding about these close situations as long as they trust the fairness of the promotion system—and the fairness and objectivity of their managers.

What if Sam Johnson, hopeful of a promotion, is the only one in his whole department doing his particular job? How can he be identified as a top producer in competition with, say, five men and women all doing some other job in his salary level? Sam, like the others, works against an EPR which is issued by the estimating department and is constantly being revised according to cumulative production experience. Here, too, the EPR becomes the standard for comparison.

But there are some jobs that just don't lend themselves to entirely quantitative measurement. Here we must introduce the distinction between "direct" and "indirect" work, a distinction that will be of major importance in later chapters of this book. At Lexington, we use the term "direct" to describe labor applied directly—*physically*—to the production and packing of the product. "Indirect" is everything else: shipping, parts handling, accounting, secretarial and clerical work, and everyone in the front office from the receptionists to the general manager. They don't physically work on the product.

Jobs that are 100 percent direct are, almost without exception, subject to objective measurement, by simple counting of pieces handled. In our Office Products Division, the more remote a job is from producing the product, the harder it is to rate it objectively. But we try. We analyze those factors of each job that are essential to it and try to develop objective measures: inquiries handled, inventory forms completed, invoices paid, interviews conducted, and so forth. Subjective judgments must enter: for example, neatness and legibility of inventory records, telephone courtesy by someone who makes public contact, ability to produce and convey complete information. We will never arrive at a completely objective system for judging the productivity of "indirects," but we emphasize the aspects of their work that *can* be measured objectively. This policy makes each person, whether direct or indirect, feel that effective performance of his or her job is the sole basis for promotions—and that judgments are made as fairly as possible.

Outsiders are sometimes amazed at the lengths to which we go to strengthen our system of objectivity regarding promotions. For example, we debated long and hard over whether absenteeism should be considered. We decided it shouldn't, concluding that the causes of absenteeism were something the personnel department might want to investigate but that this issue was separate from a person's productivity.

More recently, however, we've become convinced that the question of absenteeism is more complicated. If a person is indeed ill, with corroboration by a doctor, his absence can't be held against him, and his production record should be adjusted accordingly. If he needed time off for personal reasons and took it with the advance consent of management, that can't be held against him or his production record. But when a person has a record of chronic absenteeism, we've decided that the proper way to evaluate him is by judging his production level over a longer span of time—perhaps 24 or 36 weeks instead of 12. If he still comes out top producer, he has earned his promotion and raise in pay. We are constantly looking for refinements of that sort to guarantee that our system is fair to both the producer and the company.

When a person has gone through the considerable discipline —mental as well as physical—of becoming a top producer, what has he earned a promotion *to?* The next higher job on the assembly line? Most often, yes. That's usually the job he's had his eye on, the one that motivated his sustained achievement. And he deserves it.

But sometimes that isn't the job he wants at all—and he should be able to turn it down without prejudicing his earned right to a promotion. Knowing he's a top producer, he may go up to his manager one day and say, "When a job in the salary level above mine opens up in the toolroom (or, for that matter, in engineering or the front office), I'd like to have a crack at it." It's his manager's duty to look for such an opening and give that man his chance if possible. At our plant, even if the transfer requires training him from scratch, we are prepared—in fact, eager—to train him. (The only exception would be if the training required some unusual degree of technical preparation.) Experience has shown us time and again that an outstanding achiever in one job is likely to be a rapid learner in another job he really wants.

Career paths are bunk. The idea that a person must rise up through an organization in a straight line is a notion held by limited-minded managers who perceive everyone else as limited too.

We had a woman who had become a top producer as a carriage adjuster in Level 17. In her first few years in our plant she had earned 19 pay increases. Nearly every month, her salary went up by about two dollars a week. A Level 18 job opened on the line. She said she didn't want it. For one thing, it required a lot of lifting of whole typewriters. Besides, she wanted to broaden her work experience. Her manager canvassed other opportunities at Level 18 in far-flung departments, and showed her a list of a dozen or so jobs that were

*need for
Co. to let
their
employees
know.
be
aware*

open or might soon be open. The woman was amazed. She had
not realized the wide variety of work done in our large plant.
Moreover, she hadn't really believed she'd be considered eligible for so many jobs.

It turned out that she had some artistic talent she was eager
to use. Her manager arranged for creation of a half-time job
in engineering, in which the woman assisted engineers by
making drawings. For the remaining half of her time, she
stayed in her old job as a carriage adjuster at the top pay
rate. This arrangement produced an interesting side benefit.
Less fatigued because she was spending only half a day on
the assembly line, she began to adjust more carriages per hour
than she previously had as the best carriage adjuster on the
line. Still another side benefit: Her peers were motivated to
do better work upon seeing the opportunity she had earned.

We have promoted top producers on the assembly line into
the education department for employee training, into production control, and into clerical jobs. Another woman, formerly
a final adjuster, is now supervising a typing pool. That's what
she wanted—and, as a top producer, she had earned a right
to the opportunity.

One of our top-producing toolmakers once announced to
his manager that he'd like to transfer to accounting. He'd
been studying accounting on his own and wanted to change
careers. We decided that an intelligent man who had learned
the fine points of toolmaking could learn accounting too. At
any rate, he'd earned his right to try. Today this man is a
project manager in our accounting office. In fact, he has become an expert on inventory, which in our business is extremely complex—thousands of part numbers and millions of
parts, which are distributed among our worldwide plants,
among subassembly contractors, among warehouses, and so on.
When our other plants get into inventory trouble, this man—
this former toolmaker—is usually the one we send to help
straighten things out.

Sometimes I'm asked whether this system results in managers subtly blocking the path of top producers who want to transfer to another department. After all, no manager likes to lose one of his best people; he'd much rather see the person promoted up through his own department. For 15 years we've been drumming into our managers that our interests—and *their* interests—are best served by each person achieving his ambition as a reward for top production. By letting a top producer move up and away, thus creating upward movement in his own department, the manager motivates everyone else. Conversely, if he stands in that person's way, his entire department's morale will sink—and so will production.

Here is a case where we verified that theory dramatically, and on a broad scale. When production began on the Selectric typewriter, we filled the key production jobs by moving in *all* the top producers from the typebar assembly line, promoting them to the next salary level and training them for their new work. Then we filled the vacancies on the typebar line (which were the most advanced jobs) with people from lower-skill jobs on that line. Finally, we filled the bottom jobs for both products with newly hired people.

That was a tremendous upward movement of people. My cost-control man came to me with a slide rule and a worried face, predicting disaster for the typebar typewriter because of the sudden loss of all its top producers. What would happen to our production cost? It would kill us! Of course, he was assuming that a person's productivity is static, that everyone's rate would remain what it had been before. As it turned out, production-line people got so fired up by their new promotions that in the next year we took more time off the manufacture of the typebar typewriter than we'd done in any previous year.

What do we do when a vacancy occurs in first-line management? Does a top producer get that, too? Absolutely yes. Of course, several top producers will be considered; perhaps the top producer in every top-level job in the area. Granted, some subjective judgment will be exercised here. Is the candidate strong on winning the confidence and respect of other people? Is he an effective communicator? At this level of promotion, we also check and compare personnel files—looking at education, experience, and other factors.

But we have learned to distrust our own prejudgments, and to struggle against them. At a meeting once, one of our managers said, "I've got the world's best welder, but he'll never make a manager. He just doesn't have it." That kind of remark crushes me. I said, "Don't *ever* tell me that you *know* a man won't make a manager without trying him. Why do you think he's been working his heart out?" That world's-best-welder got his promotion, and has since risen to become a project manager.

A top producer in any job has earned the right to test himself in a better job. That is basic to what we believe in.

FULL EMPLOYMENT

Some people in American industry have the impression that IBM never fires anyone. That's not quite true. When a person fails at one job, we try him in another, and if necessary in still another. We also coach and counsel him in any way we can. But we do fire people for incompetence or for serious infractions of work rules. In our Lexington plant of 6,000 IBMers, we have six to a dozen occasions a year to separate someone from the company.

Since its inception, however, IBM has followed a practice that we call full employment. To my knowledge, we have never been forced to lay off people for lack of work to do. This has remained true during periods of sharp business dips, during periods of retooling, and so forth. The convenience of the company is not a valid reason for putting a person out of work.

Steady, secure, year-round employment can be planned by good management. It is, in fact, a duty of management. There's a fairly simple way to make any manager highly creative in planning steady employment for all his people. Just ask him to take this pledge: "If I manage (or mismanage) my plant in such a way as to have to lay off someone for lack of work, I'll be the first person laid off."

Is the practice of full employment costly? Sometimes yes—in the short run. But for the long run, other questions have to be asked. Have our systems of merit pay, merit promotion, and work simplification been profitable? All these motivational methods to increase productivity—especially work simplification, to be described in the next chapter—would be so much wheel-spinning without the foundation of full employment. Why?

By setting our sights on higher productivity, we are asking people to turn out more goods in less time. If possible, we'd like last year's 40 hours of production to be turned out next year in 30 hours. Better still, we'd like every producer to think up ways of eliminating his work altogether—and we've had people gladly and ingeniously do just that.

But there's only one way we can ask people to strive toward that goal. They must be absolutely assured that by eliminating their work they are not eliminating *themselves*—or anyone else. They must know, without doubt, that elimination of work will bring not a penalty but a reward—higher pay and increased opportunity for promotion. If there came a time when we laid off people for lack of work, how could we ever convince IBMers that we have a common interest in trying to put out more goods in less time? That is why job security—full employment—is the foundation of increased productivity.

In that light, let's examine the practice of full employment and how we make it work. There are two problems: (1) the uncertainty surrounding new products, (2) unexpected changes in demand.

Suppose we're starting production on a new model of typewriter or on a new product. We have to go through the complex calculations, familiar to most manufacturing managers, of deciding how many of the new product we can risk producing, how much machinery we'll have to install to produce them, and how many production people to assign to the new venture. The techniques involved in those calculations could occupy a book by themselves. What we're concerned with here is the "people" part of the question: how to insure the job security of the people we assign, despite the uncertainties of our future production demand.

Two main elements go into these calculations: (1) keeping the initial labor force as *lean* as possible until product acceptance is assured, and (2) a system of *buffers* to soften the impact of the unexpected. Actually, these two elements somewhat overlap, and are the same elements that are built into the annual operating plan to insure job security.

The first tool we use is *overtime*, which is a buffer against the unexpected and, at the same time, a way to keep the labor force lean. A new product is subject to many ups and downs. People are on a learning curve—not only assemblers but parts-manufacturing people, managers, and suppliers—and sometimes their efficiency increases unevenly. At the same time, product demand, as transmitted by sales-department orders, travels a bumpy road. Use of overtime gives us considerable leeway in stepping up or stepping down production without adding new production people or having to reassign them elsewhere. We build into our plans a normal allowance of 10 to 12 overtime Saturdays a year, which our people are requested to work as it becomes necessary, and we may expand overtime up to 22 Saturdays. Since this plan gives us the option of scheduling no Saturday overtime at all, we have considerable

flexibility in varying our man-days per year without altering
the number of people in our work force.

The second buffer is to *lengthen our delivery schedule.*
Normally we deliver a typewriter within two to four weeks
of an order, if the machine has no unusual requirements. During peak periods or after introduction of new models, we
sometimes stretch delivery time to 12 or even 16 weeks, so as
to transfer the heavy manufacturing demands to valley periods. Needless to say, this may be inconvenient to the customer or may even endanger a sale, neither of which we like
to do. But we accept that risk for the sake of full employment,
to which we attach a higher priority.

Our third major stabilizing device is a large warehouse for
consigning our typewriter inventory. During business dips,
we have consigned as many as 50,000 typewriters to the
shelf. At active times, we've gone as low as only a couple of
thousand waiting to be shipped. Thus, employment can remain
steady through the peaks and dips of customer demand.

A fourth buffer is enabled by *subcontracting.* During work
dips, we sometimes resort to doing our own job machining of
parts that we might ordinarily subcontract, giving us an additional minor buffer. We make considerable use of outside job
shops, usually for the machining of parts made by standard
equipment. Job shops, like printers or neighborhood doctors,
are set up to provide service as needed, on an order-by-order
basis. They stabilize their work flow through having a broad
range of customers.

On the subject of subcontracting, it is worth noting that
most of our buffers also buffer our regular experienced and
tooled subcontractors, who are mostly in the field of subassemblies. In 17 years at Lexington, we have experienced
some big swings in demand, yet these swings have had little
effect on our regular subcontractors.

We use other minor buffers which have their counterparts
in almost any business. A certain amount of our production

goes to supply our own salesmen with demonstrators and to be used within the far-flung offices of IBM. That gives us another small buffer. Whenever possible, we schedule work on the inside-IBM demand so as to level off our dips. Also, during slack periods we temporarily transfer some people to the work of reconditioning salesmen's demonstrators and machines received as trade-ins; these reconditioned machines are sold to schools and to dealers in used office equipment.

Finally, we have a major buffer that is reserved for extreme and prolonged cases of demand dip, one that is available only to sizable companies that have diversified products. Even in times of general business recession, a company like IBM has one or more products, usually new ones, for which the demand is expanding. What we have done on occasion is to move some of the manufacturing of those high-demand products to a plant whose regular products are in temporary trouble. Such a transfer, of course, is expensive and can seldom be justified purely on a cost basis. But we consider it imperative on a people basis. Having hired a work force for a particular plant, the company is obligated to provide work for that force. This is one of the costs that may sometimes be incurred to keep full employment a *practice*, not a theory. To have the benefits of a full employment practice, it is simply necessary to pay certain costs.

We estimate that these buffers, used with sensitive foresight and planning, permit us to absorb the shock of as much as a 25 percent decrease in demand without invoking the extreme step of moving a product from one plant to another for employment reasons.

When it does appear that this extreme step is necessary, is the cost really worth it? I will answer in the affirmative but will not argue my case on the basis of social responsibility (though I do have strong feelings on this subject). I'll just point to the statistics cited in the Introduction to this book: Our people, by using their minds as well as their hands, have cut two-thirds of the hours that go into manufacturing our typewriter. The cost of the product went down 45 percent during a ten-year period when wages vastly increased. That achievement would have been impossible without productive and committed employees. And much of their commitment stems from the security they know is theirs through IBM's practice of full employment.

WORK SIMPLIFICATION
TRAINING

All the incentives and productivity devices described in this book are a package—interdependent. Yet if I had to single out one program most directly responsible for our productivity increase—moving our division from no profit to healthy profit —the choice would have to be work simplification.

Essentially work simplification is an education program, but it is an action program as well. Extremely well received by our people, its benefits go on, year after year. The success of this program is, at least to me, living proof that people deeply want to make a personal contribution, to be recognized for it, and to be tangibly rewarded for it. Their natural inclination is to see their own security as tied to the health and security of their company—as long as the company does not force company interest and personal interest into opposition with each other.

Before describing our work-simplification program in detail, let's look at the historical setting from which it arose, as well as a personal experience or two.

Shortly after World War II, industrial engineering entered its heyday. As a young manager, I was given a chance in 1946 to attend New York University's first roundtable in industrial efficiency. The course was a revelation; I had not known that the simplification of work was a science. But it threw me into conflict. On the one hand, having been an assembler for 13 years, I thought, "If I'd known all these things earlier, how much more work I could have gotten done." On the other hand, I had seen—in fact, had felt—how assemblers react to time-study engineers and their stopwatches. They resent being told how to move their hands and having those movements timed in split seconds. Nothing in manufacturing is more degrading to the individual. The assembler's main reaction to the time-study man is a desire to get rid of him—preferably by a kick to the seat of his pants.

As technical and rich in specifics as that NYU course was, I saw nothing in it that was beyond the comprehension of any assembler of reasonable intelligence. How could an assembler take full advantage of the ideas contained in the course without having some "expert" shove it down his throat?

Let's dwell a moment on the theoretical approach to time and motion study. The "expert"—who is expected to analyze any job in the shop but has probably never performed any of them himself—breaks down each job into motions, figures out a sequence of motions that is supposed to be most efficient, and then times them. The right hand must reach ten inches for a part—the industrial engineer marks that down on a sheet. Then he looks in the book to see how long it takes to move the right hand ten inches. The right hand must grasp the part and put it into place. He looks in the book twice—once for grasping and once for putting something into place. Then the left hand must reach for a part. This time the IE turns to a different page in the book, because the left hand takes a little longer than the right hand. If the assembler is left-handed, all the figures have to be reversed. When the job has been completely analyzed, the times are added up and the production rate is set. There was once even a rate set for moving the eyeballs.

Time study, whether theoretical or actual, leads to a war of nerves and wits. For example, in the assembly area where I worked in the 1930s, we had stopwatch time studies for a while. Now and then we'd find a part that didn't fit right. We'd throw each ill-fitting part into a back corner of its stock bin, and after a while we had a pretty good inventory of parts that wouldn't fit. We had a fellow named Frank, a terrific assembler, who often completed a normal day's work before the morning was out. Then he'd go to the restroom and read a newspaper for an hour or two. One day our manager caught Frank in the middle of the sports page. I overheard him on the phone a minute later, calling the time-study man and fuming, "We've got a rate up here that's all wrong! You've got to take a look at it."

As I recall, Frank's work was rated at 65¢ per piece. The time-study man rushed upstairs with his book, clipboard, and stopwatch. For two days he timed Frank. But meanwhile Frank had hauled out of the back of the bins his hoard of parts that wouldn't fit. As he worked, he filed or bent or fitted them into place. Finally, the time-study man reported to the manager, "You were right. Frank's time was all wrong. It's not a 65¢ job. It's got to be 85¢." The manager hit the ceiling, but the time-study man had all the elements in black and white. They finally compromised on 75¢—and after a few days, Frank went back to reading his newspaper.

That's the way companies used to "motivate" people—and the way some still do.

In 1958, twelve years after I took the NYU course, I was able to start resolving the conflict I felt about it. We had recently opened the Lexington plant, and two of our top managers went to NYU for a similar course. They, in turn, conducted 40 hours of training for every manager in the plant. That got us ready to try an experiment.

We decided that (1) a person who does a job knows that job better than any expert, and (2) work performed only by a person's hands—without the use of his mind as well—is a sheer waste of talent. What would happen if we helped people become their own industrial engineers? The basic principles of motion efficiency were not beyond the comprehension of anyone in our plant. After learning these principles, if each person were to decide for himself how to do his job better, he'd *really* do it better.

We selected an experimental group of low-, medium-, and high-productivity people and gave them a 21-hour course. We then kept a close watch on what happened to their productivity. After the first few weeks, in which our most hopeful expectations were exceeded, we decided to pull out all stops. Tightening the course down to 15 hours—3 hours a day for 5 days—we scheduled work-simplification training for every person in the plant. With several classes of 20 going simultaneously, we would reach everyone within two and a half years.

SESSION 1

In the first session we presented, with the aid of charts and projectors, a detailed history of work from the building of the pyramids through the spinning jenny, the cotton gin, steam and electric engines, child labor laws, the time-and-motion-study principles of Frederick W. Taylor and the Gilbreths, the mass production principles of Henry Ford, and finally our own "participation principle": *No one knows the job like the person doing it. Everyone is trained in work simplification, from the general manager to the newest person hired.*

This was followed by discussion and self-testing in psychological resistance to change. We then had everyone play the role of a customer who was comparing our product with those of competitors, to point up the need for saving time and cutting costs through work simplification. Next, we presented and discussed this five-step plan for approaching any job improvement:

1. *Record all details of your job.* Here we introduced various fact-finding charts to be taken up later in the course: flow process chart, flow diagram, right-hand and left-hand chart, multicolumn flow process chart, man-and-machine chart.

2. *Pick a worthwhile problem in doing your job.* Examples: bottlenecks, waste motions, poor sequence of operations.

3. *Question with an open mind.* In recording each detail, ask *What? Where? When? Who? How?*—and, above all, *Why?* Rudyard Kipling once said that those six words taught him everything he knew.

4. *Develop an improvement.* An improvement may be achieved by simplifying the steps, combining the steps, changing the place, changing the sequence of the steps, or, best of all, eliminating the steps altogether.

5. *Install the improvement.* This involves "selling" it by clearly presenting it (to manager, co-workers, etc.) with details fully worked out; conducting a trial run; giving credit to everyone connected with the improvement; following up to make sure the improvement is applied correctly; and standardizing it, i.e., looking for all possible applications that will help get full mileage out of the improvement.

Finally, Session 1 ends with a summary of the objectives of work simplification: learning new thinking tools, producing a better product or service, cutting costs, reducing fatigue, enhancing teamwork, increasing job satisfaction, and, perhaps most attractive of all, increasing personal income through (a) a suggestion award, (b) a merit increase, (c) a special recognition award, or (d) productivity credit toward promotion into a more responsible, higher-paying position.

SESSION 2

The next session began by showing the class members how to draw up a flow process chart. Such a chart is used to record everything done by a person or done to a material in a single job. Basically each step is classified as an operation, a transportation, an inspection, a delay, or a storage, with a standard symbol used for each. Figures 1a and 1b are examples of the type of flow process chart we used.

In introducing these charts, we also introduced the concept of a "do" operation as against a "make-ready" or "putaway" operation. Upon seeing his job in terms of these breakdowns, a person may become aware for the first time that he is performing 16 steps of make-ready, perhaps walking 115 feet, to prepare for ten seconds of *doing*. Obviously the potential for saving time is in all that make-ready. Without this analysis, his natural tendency would probably have been to try to cut time off the "doing" part of the operation.

Flow diagrams, similar to the standard ones known to most managers, appear in Figures 2a and 2b. These are diagrammatic representations of the steps in Figures 1a and 1b.

SESSION 3

In Session 3, a film entitled *Principles of Motion Economy* is shown and cards are distributed listing 20 of those principles:

1. Move hands simultaneously.
2. Use symmetrical motions.
3. Use rotary wrist motions.
4. Shift muscle tensions.
5. Work within arm's length.
6. Move arms in circular paths.
7. Slide, don't carry.
8. Have a fixed place for everything.
9. Perform make-ready work in batches.
10. Use rhythm and automaticity.

Figure 1a. Flow process chart—present.

IBM

OFFICE PRODUCTS DIVISION

FLOW PROCESS CHART 841-1303-1 PAGE 1 OF 1

PART OR FORM NO.	OPERATION NO.	PART NAME OR FORM NAME
VARIOUS		DIE CAST COVERS

OPERATION DESCRIPTION: MOVEMENT OF COVERS (TRUCKLOAD OF 512 = 32 PALLETS) TO PLANT,
TO PAINT VENDOR, THEN TO OUR FINAL ASSEM. LINE

SUMMARY	PRESENT NO. TIME	PROPOSED NO. TIME	DIFFERENCE NO. TIME
OPERATIONS	4		
TRANSPORTATIONS	12 521		
INSPECTIONS	4 232		
DELAYS	3		
STORAGES			
DISTANCE TRAVELLED	82,570 FT.	FT.	FT.

☐ MAN OR ☑ MATERIAL DIE CAST COVERS
CHART BEGINS TRAILER AT OUR REC. DOCK
CHART ENDS OUR FINAL ASSEM. LINE
DATE ____

DETAILS OF (PRESENT) METHOD	DIST. IN FEET	QUANTITY	TIME MIN.	NOTES	
1. UNLOADED TO DOCK		50 PER PALLET	1/2	REPEATED FOR 32 PALLETS. FORK TRUCK	
2. COUNTED, CHECKED B/L			10	REC. CLERK	
3. MOVED TO REC. INSP. AREA	200		1	REPEAT 32 TIMES	
4. AWAIT INSPECTION					
5. INSPECTED (SAMPLE)			30	REC. INSP.	
6. MOVED TO SHIP. DOCK	250		1 1/2	REPEAT 32 TIMES	
7. AWAIT SHIP.					
8. LOADED ON TRUCK	400		6	HAND TRUCK — REPEATED	
9. TRUCKED TO PAINT VENDOR	3000		10	8 PAL./TRIP — FOUR	
10. PAINTED COVERS RETURNED TO PLANT	3000		10	" — TIMES	
11. UNLOADED, REC. DOCK	400		6		
12. COUNTED, ETC.			3	REC. CLERK. FORK LIFT. REPEAT 32 TIMES	
13. MOVED TO REC. INSP.	200		1		
14. AWAIT 100% PRINT INSPECTION					
15. INSPECTED, PLACED IN CARTS		92	180	21⁺ CARTS OF (24). REC. INSP.	
16. MOVED TO DROP AREA	800		8	FORK LIFT — REPEATED	
17. PUSHED TO ELEVATOR	250		2	ASSEM. CLERK — 21⁺	
18. MOVED TO SECOND FLOOR	20		1	ASSEM. CLERK — TIMES	
19. PUSHED TO FINAL ASSEM. AREA	200		2	ASSEM. CLERK	
20. USED BY ASSEMBLER		512			
21.					

PLEASE PRINT NAME	DEPT. NO.	MAN NO.	SIGNATURE

11. Use foot pedal when possible.
12. Use holding devices.
13. Arrange for orderly disposal.
14. Use ejectors.
15. Shorten transport distance.
16. Pre-position product.
17. Pre-position tools and supplies.
18. Locate machine controls.
19. Improve workplace height.
20. Improve conditions of light, heat, dust, etc.

Before the film is shown and the list distributed, however, the class is put through a simple experience to dramatize mo-

Figure 1b. Flow process chart—proposed.

tion economy. A plastic bag containing a pegboard and pegs is given to each of ten pairs of partners. While one partner is to record time, the other partner is instructed to remove the pegboard from the bag and insert the pegs into holes as fast as he can. No other instructions are given.

After the film, each pair is asked to analyze the pegboard assignment in view of all the principles of motion economy that might apply. They are given time to work out improved

Figure 2a. Flow diagram—present.

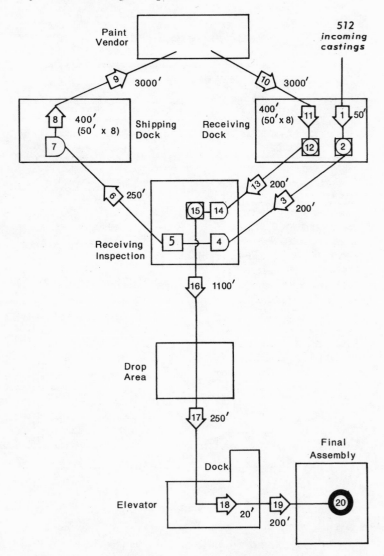

techniques and practice them. Then they time their new method, giving the instructor their best time out of two or three tries. The obvious improvement then leads the way into

Figure 2b. Flow diagram—proposed.

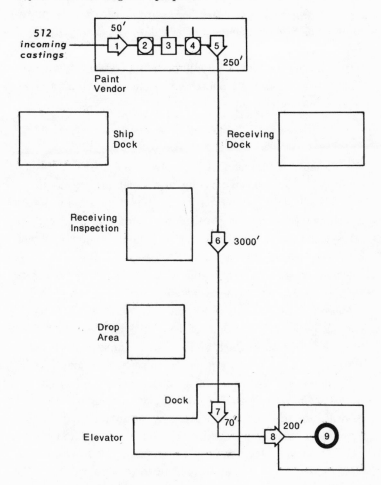

discussion of the actual jobs of class members and techniques for improving their performance.

SESSION 4

This session gets into the more sophisticated multicolumn flow chart, which charts the flow of several pieces of material and their relationships, instead of the single material followed by the flow process chart. After learning to construct the multicolumn chart, class members discuss how the chart helps spot duplications and bottlenecks and helps find ways to combine two or more operations and eliminate unnecessary operations. Again, lessons learned from the multicolumn chart are applied to examination of people's actual jobs.

SESSION 5

In Session 5, class members are introduced to the additional thinking tools of brainstorming and attribute listing. Using all the analysis tools learned during the week, class members now intensively apply these tools to redesigning their regular jobs—charting new ways to perform old tasks, trying them, perfecting them, and recharting them.

There were a few major differences in the courses given to office people and the courses given to machine-shop people.

Office people and others classified as "indirects" (or supporting personnel) concentrated on analyzing what happens to a piece of paper. Each piece of paper creates work, often spawning dozens of other pieces of paper. For example, what happens as a consequence of an order to buy a certain material? It may lead to freight bills, inspection reports, test records, an invoice from the vendor, an account payable, an approval to pay, and a check to the vendor. Is all that paperwork really necessary to keep a business going? What needs really *must* be served, and how can they be served with the fewest pieces of paper and in the least time? The class for "indirects" also dwelt on how to be precise and clear in communication—how to write a letter in the simplest way.

This training program in analysis of record keeping eventually gave rise to a major program to increase our productivity. The latter program, called Simplified Business Procedures, will be detailed in later chapters.

The machine-shop class focused on the man-machine relationship, using a man-machine chart. The machinist produces parts, often on an extremely expensive machine—for example, a transfer machine that costs $2 million. Idleness of the machine for seconds or minutes, while the man is doing something with his hands or fetching material, costs far more than idleness of the man while the machine is doing its work. If the man has to move something, or measure something or check something, how can his task be done while the machine is doing its work, so that both partners, the man and machine, work at maximum productivity?

The slogan that emerged from the work-simplification classes was *Work Smarter, Not Harder*. Our aim was a speedup of production, not a speedup of human beings. People discovered that by using their minds they could fashion all sorts of shortcuts while continuing to work at their accustomed pace—and they got immense satisfaction out of their discoveries. Once introduced to the idea that a human hand is too valuable to use as a holding device, they invented dozens of simple holding fixtures. We assured people that they could rearrange their workplaces any way they wished, and that we would provide any devices and tools they needed that would reduce lost motion and fatigue.

Early in our work-simplification program, we had to face a difficult question. We had already decided that anyone coming up with a cost-saving idea would receive a suggestion award. (At first the award equaled 10 percent of a year's estimated net savings. Over the years we have gradually raised this cash award to 20 percent.) The question, however, was whether the person's increased productivity, brought about by his idea, should also be counted toward a merit increase in pay and toward promotion. We decided the answer had to be yes. Our whole philosophy is that we don't care how he improves his productivity as long as he does it. All the better if he does it by introducing a procedural improvement, because that improvement can probably be passed on to his co-workers and his successors, thus becoming a permanent improvement. That's a far more valuable contribution than merely speeding up production by sweating harder.

WORK SIMPLIFICATION
THE PAYOFF

Input is one thing; output another. The preceding chapter described the "input" of work simplification—the theory and training aimed at developing greater involvement and higher productivity. What has been the "output"—the actual improvements people have contributed to manufacturing procedures, the reduction in costs, the changes in less tangible but somewhat measurable areas like working attitudes and degree of involvement?

Before summing up and evaluating the entire program, let's first take a sampling of the work-simplification ideas devised by IBMers after they were trained to become their own industrial engineers.

One man received a $2,600 suggestion award—and saved the company many times that amount—for what may be the shortest written suggestion on record. Working in the chemical production area for our Copier, he wrote, "Move the vibrascrew and recycle-tank forward to eliminate loss of toner material." That suggestion, without so much as a diagram, clearly communicated a simple solution to a costly problem.

Another example: A man working on a subassembly for the electric typewriter used to attach a supporting bar to an aluminum basket casting, cut the bar down to a neat fit, throw the excess away—then stand and wait for the next casting. Several places up the line, an operator of a multiple-spindle drilling machine, having become more observant after his work-simplification course, suggested, "Why cut that bar down there? Leave it on until it gets to me. I have time open while my drilling machine is doing its job. If you move the cutoff machine next to me, I can take on that job while I'm waiting." So the cutoff man was freed for another assignment—and the man who had the idea was given a percentage of his annual salary as a reward.

Still another person, who broached the ratchets for the typewriter platen, saw a clear opportunity after he drew up his man-machine chart in class and analyzed it. He perceived that the operation following his was wirebrushing. He suggested, "If we put the wirebrush next to the broach, I can easily wirebrush the burrs off the part while the broach is running." Again, two jobs were combined into one.

But that fellow, spurred by his cash award and, it's fair to say, pride in his ingenuity, still had free time while his machine worked. He noticed that the operation after the wirebrushing was stamping a part number on the ratchet. He told his manager, "If you want to put that stamping machine here, I can do the part number too." Now obviously, if someone else—a manager or engineer—had tried to foist these extra jobs on that man he would probably have responded with all sorts of resistance, including obstinate proof that one man couldn't do all those jobs. But enticed by the possibilities of cash awards, increases in salary, and sharply increased opportunity for promotion, he eagerly sought improvements that an engineer might not find—or wouldn't dare suggest if he did find.

Were the increased duties taken on by that man a contradiction of our slogan "Work smarter, not harder"? Not at all. He sensed that his previous single task left too much of his reserve untapped. He could dip deeply into his reserve without undue fatigue—and we carefully observed his combination of tasks to make sure they could be sustained without strain, either to himself or to anyone of reasonable competence who might replace him. That man can be expected to keep coming up with new and better ideas. He has experienced, in both creative satisfaction and cold cash, the rewards of using mental abilities that in most factory jobs he would never have been invited to employ.

In the first four years after we introduced work-simplification training (between 1958 and 1962), suggestions from people in the machining area alone produced 62 job combinings, most of them fully releasing a man for another job.

For every one of these spectacular suggestions, there were dozens of simpler but still valuable ones: "Replace conventional stripping tank in paint department with sludge-settling tank. This will facilitate cleaning of tanks" (an estimated saving of $6,385; cash award, $985). "Relocate cutoff tools in raw stores closer to material storage areas. This will reduce distance of walking and carrying materials, reduce fatigue and exposure to accidents" (savings, $4,665; award, $760). One person suggested a rearrangement of work stations on the automatic cam lever assembly machine to provide better flow (savings, $7,608; award, $1,200). Among indirects, one man proposed and designed portable desks for clerks in the receiving department; clerks now move their desks to where the job is, eliminating time wasted walking from the receiving area to the receiving office for filling out reports (savings, $11,883; award, $1,810). And thousands upon thousands of awards have been made in the range of a few hundred dollars or less.

In June 1962 we drew up our first major summary of suggestion awards and savings. At that time the 2,700 people eligible for suggestion awards had altogether submitted more than 2,000 projects, of which roughly 500 were found acceptable. We were able to show firm documentation for savings of 122,000 manhours and $27,000 in materials.

Did this explosion of ideas taper off after the early burst of excitement?

In 1965 alone, suggestion submissions totaled 9,600—and 2,600 were found worthy of acceptance. Savings that year amounted to $835,000, of which $181,000 was paid out as awards to 1,425 people (out of 3,300 eligible). Note the high degree of participation: Three out of four eligible people turned in at least one suggestion. The total number of suggestions submitted, 9,600, was almost three times the number of eligible people, 3,300. And out of 2,445 people participating, 1,425 received at least one award.

By 1972 we had broadened eligibility to include more people, for a total of 5,539. They submitted 12,000 suggestions, of which 3,400 were accepted, from almost 2,900 different participants (more than half of those eligible). They received $270,000 in awards for producing savings of $1,130,000.

Where is the plant whose industrial engineering experts can match that dollars-and-cents progress in productivity—not to mention the feeling of participation, responsibility, and career opportunity that spreads even to the newest, least skilled assembler?

Of course, launching the plantwide course in work simplification was an expensive risk, amounting to three or four hundred thousand dollars. At its peak it required a staff of seven people, three of them full- or part-time instructors and the rest working to generate and expedite evaluation of suggestions. But the biggest cost by far was the investment of 65,000 manhours in class.

Did it pay out? It certainly did—with an immediacy that astounded us.

For one thing, the manhours "lost"—15 hours per week per student—didn't seem to be lost at all. We were careful to select the 20 students per class from a wide distribution of departments to avoid creating bottlenecks. The end-of-month production reports by managers showed no dip in products turned out. It seems that students, steamed up by their three-hour class, produced their normal daily quota in what was left of their day, or perhaps their co-workers on the line filled in while students were at class. So in that sense the biggest cost—the classes—actually cost nothing.

But the big payout was in the ideas that emerged from the classes. Every single class we have conducted has *more than paid for itself* by generating money-saving ideas—before the classes were even completed. By 1962 we had invested 65,000 manhours in the first go-round of classes. Those people had already produced ideas that saved 122,000 hours of unnecessary work, not to mention saved materials.

That is why work simplification has become a permanent way of life in our Lexington plant. Every newly hired person is given the work-simplification course, usually between six months and a year after he joins us—not so soon as to confuse him, but not so late as to have allowed him to get too set in his ways. Also, every few years "old" graduates are given a short refresher course.

Near the end of the first full round of classes, we took an attitude survey about them. Of those surveyed, 84 percent had attended a class and 16 percent had not yet done so.

We knew at the outset that work simplification was not a panacea for work improvement or morale or anything else, and many respondents reminded us of that. But the results were heavily positive and quite gratifying. Here is a brief summary:

Not a Panacea

How would you rate the program?

Good or very good	72%
So-so	17
Poor or very poor	4
Don't know anything about it	7

Has it helped or hurt the AMOUNT of work you do?

Helped	63%
Hurt	0
Neither	37

Has it helped or hurt the QUALITY of work you do?

Helped	45%
Hurt	1
Neither	54

Has it helped or hurt the METHODS by which you do your work?

Helped	73%
Hurt	1
Neither	26

Has it helped or hurt the fairness in the amount of work expected of you?

Helped	28%
Hurt	2
Neither	70

Has it helped or hurt the number of suggestions you have submitted?

Helped	49%
Hurt	3
Neither	48

Has it helped or hurt the quality of your suggestions?

Helped	51%
Hurt	2
Neither	47

Has it helped or hurt the cooperation between you and your fellow employees?

Helped	39%
Hurt	1
Neither	60

Has it helped or hurt understanding your job?

Helped	59%
Hurt	0
Neither	41

Has it helped or hurt how tired you feel at the end of the day?

Helped	29%
Hurt	3
Neither	68

Has it helped or hurt your manager's awareness of trouble spots (such as tool trouble, lack of work, lack of manpower, etc.)?

Helped	47%
Hurt	2
Neither	51

Has it helped or hurt the amount of "say" employees have in deciding which methods to use in their work?

Helped	62%
Hurt	1
Neither	37

When you were being trained in work simplification, how well did you understand the material that was presented?

Very well	59%
Fairly well	39
Not too well	2
Didn't understand at all	0

Did you receive enough training or would you have preferred more?

Enough, but would like more	68%
Would have preferred a little more	25
Would have preferred a lot more	7

The weight in many of the above responses lies with the neutral answer, in most cases "neither." This may seem to contradict my observation that the results were heavily positive. But it should be pointed out that for several of these questions the neutral answer is really a positive one—and, in fact, provides evidence that respondents were making careful discriminations. For example, after responding heavily that the training helped the *amount* of work, more than half the respondents said the training neither helped nor hurt the *quality* of their work. That is a most heartening answer. The course was not directed at improving quality. The responses assure us that only one out of a hundred felt that the increased *amount* of work—the actual aim of the course—had an adverse effect on quality.

An especially important question was, "Has it helped or hurt the fairness in the amount of work expected of you?" That 28 percent said "helped" is very pleasing. But that 70 percent said "neither" is even more so. The survey shows that overwhelmingly—98 percent—people think it perfectly fair to be expected to produce more work if they are properly trained to do so and are rewarded for it.

Another critical question was, "Has it helped or hurt the cooperation between you and your fellow employees?" Some people argue against work-simplification training on the ground that it invites dog-eat-dog competition between employees, especially since it may reward one person for eliminating another's accustomed job. Apparently, our graduates disagree—by 99 percent. Sixty percent say it neither helps nor hurts, and 39 percent say it helps cooperation.

The most frequent argument we hear from outsiders against our various incentive programs—merit pay and promotion as well as work simplification—is that they may reward people for speeding themselves up to the point of excessive fatigue. Our counterargument is our slogan: We want people to work smarter, not harder. Therein lies the importance of the 68 percent who said "neither" to the question "Has it helped or hurt how tired you feel at the end of the day?" Twenty-nine percent of the respondents said the course in working smarter helped them *avoid* fatigue. Only 3 percent said it hurt.

Where the bulk of the answers was decidedly *un*neutral— and most gratifying—was to the question "Has it helped or hurt the amount of 'say' employees have in deciding which methods to use in their work?'' Sixty-two percent said it had helped. That is a major message we want to get through—that a person's methods are his own business, and that he is best qualified to choose them. Down that road lies job satisfaction. Thirty-seven percent said "neither," and only 1 percent said their say was hurt.

A final word on work simplification: Much of this chapter has dealt with employee suggestions—the value of such suggestions, awards for them, and so on. It would be possible for a resistant reader, or a not too careful reader, to misinterpret completely the meaning of what is being described here. The important thing is not the suggestion program, which is scarcely an innovation. Most major companies, including IBM, have conducted suggestion programs very much like this one since World War II. The importance of work-simplification training is in providing a *foundation* to the suggestion program. Without this training, the suggestion box is a catch-as-catch-can search for the intuitive genius who sits undiscovered along almost any assembly line. The box may find him or it may not. But a training program in work simplification is a systematic effort to evoke the accumulated experience—and mind power—that lies untapped everywhere in every manufacturing plant. The training organizes this mind power and experience. The suggestion box merely collects the ideas.

TRAINING FOR QUALITY

The work-simplification program had been so successful—in building esprit de corps as well as in taking manhours out of the manufacture of the typewriter—that we decided to follow it up by selecting another educational goal. After discussing several, we decided on teaching a systematic method for improving the quality of workmanship. This would improve the company's product reliability while improving job satisfaction.

Immediately we ran into an unexpected snag. In putting together our work-simplification course, we had drawn from the experience of many universities and companies that were teaching it for industrial engineers. When we began searching for an approach to teaching better workmanship, however, all we could find were "zero defect" programs and barrages of propaganda aimed at raising people's desire to do better work. We had tried both and were satisfied by neither. We could not find anyone in the United States teaching a systematic method for analyzing the elements of workmanship, a necessary prerequisite for improvement of quality. So our Lexington training department set about to design one.

We called our course Workmanship Analysis. Again, we planned to give it to every person in the plant, with variations in the course for office people and other supporting personnel. Again we planned to bring people together in classes of twenty, three hours a day for five days, mixing people from the assembly lines with all levels of management to produce a spirit of commonness of purpose. We had learned not to underestimate the importance of an assembler being able to say to his family and co-workers: "I'm in a class with so-and-so, my department manager. We're working on problems together."

We decided to assign the teaching to our second level of management, project managers. Here's a clarification of how our plant is organized: Each first-line manager immediately supervises an assembly line or a comparable production group. First-line managers report to a project manager (second-line), who coordinates production of major portions of a product. Project managers, in turn, report to a superintendent, who reports to the man in charge of producing the entire typebar typewriter, or the Selectric, the Copier, the dictating machine, or whatever. We had sensed that our second-line managers were becoming walled off from contact with the people who did the work. Teaching these classes would give project managers renewed day-to-day awareness of the problems facing direct production people.

Although these classes were not aimed at increasing efficiency in the usual sense, they were aimed at cost-cutting. Warranty time devoted to correcting defects, whether by our customer engineer or our repair department, is charged to manufacturing cost. If we could cut warranty service time, we would thereby reduce factory costs.

We decided that the criterion for success of our course would be improvement of *out-of-box quality*. Our products are not sold through distributors, but are delivered directly to the customer by either an IBM salesman or a customer engineer. When he unboxes and plugs in a typewriter in the presence of his customer, he—and the customer—expect the machine to operate perfectly. The slightest defect is a major embarrassment to him and the company. We had devised a quick and simple way to keep track of out-of-box quality. Out of our many branch offices in the United States—180 at the time this course was launched—a sampling of 12 reported to the plant on the quality of every machine they delivered. This constituted a large random sample of our entire production. Our goal was to reduce warranty calls for out-of-box defects, both in number and seriousness.

SESSION 1

For that reason, Session 1 of our Workmanship Analysis course began by dramatizing out-of-box quality in a most immediate way. The instructor had his class pretend to be a group of customers who had ordered some machines and were anticipating their delivery. He would then open the boxes of two or three typewriters. First thing, he would read off the serial number. Some members of the class would immediately recognize the number as one from a production run they had handled during the previous week. Tension would rise. The machine would then be put through a meticulous inspection, followed by sighs of relief—occasionally of dismay. The important thing was the drama itself—the idea that the quality of every machine is important to someone.

Then the instructor would pick up a phone and place a call to one of the reporting branch offices, asking that a customer engineer be paged on his citizen-band radio and that he call the classroom number in Lexington as soon as possible. Within ten or fifteen minutes the engineer's call would come, perhaps from a suburb of Boston or Dallas. His words would be heard through a desk talkbox. "Joe," the instructor would casually ask, "how has out-of-box quality been coming through out there?" And he'd *tell*, with any complaints being a matter of great importance to him. The impact in class would be terrific, whether of pride or otherwise. For the first time, many production people experienced, in a personal way, the meaning of quality from the other end of the business.

In that first session, I would give a short talk (I met with every one of our 170 classes over a two-year period) to convey that all of us, from the bottom of the company to the top, share responsibility for and proprietorship in the quality of our products. Then, after a short illustrated presentation on the historical evolution of precision in workmanship, the class would turn to personal participation. Class members would practice the use of two basic inspection tools, the micrometer and the dial indicator. To some, these are new skills. The others are assured by the activity that the course has "practical" importance.

Students are then introduced to forms—in a sense, tools—that they will use throughout the week in a three-step analysis of their own jobs. These tools are (1) a Workmanship Conditions Chart to help identify job conditions that justify special attention; (2) a Workmanship Analysis Chart to break down each condition into detail; (3) a Workmanship Solution Chart to help develop the best solution for each problem analyzed in the preceding chart. Examples of the charts are shown in Figures 3–5 at the end of this chapter. (They are adaptations of the forms used at IBM.)

The remainder of Session 1 is taken up with having each

Principles of Responsible Workmanship

1. *Maintain a neat and well-organized workplace* equipped with tools and fixtures kept in top condition.

2. *Develop an error-free work routine,* using the Principles of Motion Economy learned in work-simplification class.

3. *Inspect your own work regularly,* using calibrated equipment. Accept only good parts and release your own work only after you are sure that our customers can depend 100% on your workmanship.

4. *Ask for qualified help* when in doubt about instructions or when proper adjustments cannot be made.

5. *Understand the job specifications* used on your operations and keep informed on engineering changes. Ask for correction of errors. Suggest revisions which will improve the job specs.

6. *Report every problem condition promptly,* even if you don't have a solution. In addition, do submit a suggestion whenever you have a solution to offer.

7. *Learn the technical why* of your operation by finding out how it fits into and functionally affects the end product.

8. Arrange with your manager to *use model parts or special test machines to try out your ideas.* Remember, unauthorized changes in regular production can cause serious problems.

9. *Use care in handling* and packing the product so that adjustments and parts are not damaged.

10. Find out what your present workmanship level is and *set workmanship progress goals* for yourself.

person fill out the Workmanship Conditions Chart (Figure 3), as a start toward a full-scale investigation of his own job. To aid him in filling out this chart, each student is provided with a step-by-step operation description of his job as well as a photograph of his workbench and a layout drawing of his work station.

Finally, the class discusses ten principles of responsible workmanship. These are distributed in sheet form (shown) and summarized on a plastic-covered, wallet-size card.

SESSION 2

The next session begins with an explanation of the relationship between manufacturing engineering and product engineering, certain natural conflicts between these functions, and how we help resolve these conflicts at Lexington by having both functions report to the same production engineering manager. This begins insight into our system of total responsibility (see next chapter)—one manager totally responsible for all functions in producing a product, each producer responsible for the quality of his own work.

The class then turns to filling out the Workmanship Analysis Chart (Figure 4 at the end of this chapter). Completing this chart helps a person isolate and identify possible interference factors in his job, or helps him define a problem affecting quality so that he may proceed to a solution.

In addition, the class discusses and practices the care and use of assembly hand tools and gauges; sees a movie, *Critical Selectric Functions at High Speed,* which highlights precision and quality; and learns more about our reporting system for keeping management up to date on out-of-box performance. The latter is a reminder that quality workmanship is a matter of prime concern at all levels of the company.

SESSION 3

This session begins with an explanation of IBM marketing, going into more detail about the salesman's problems and approach and emphasizing that his most effective selling point is fine workmanship. This is brought to life by an actual sales demonstration in class, in which workmanship is the basis of the sales approach.

Then, in a change of topic (our education people have found it advantageous to change topics and modes of presentation to enliven the three-hour session), the class takes up the laws of probability. These laws are illustrated by showing patterns of chance in familiar games. This leads to a discussion of the specific applications of probability to inspection and quality control—why quality of mass production can be checked by inspection of, say, 1 out of 20 finished products. This is followed by a period of instruction in materials processing—hardnesses and how they are measured, plating and what constitutes a quality finish, sintered metals, and so on.

The class discusses identification of good versus bad parts after being handed two lists. One list, called "Types of Bad Parts That Operators Should Catch," gives different types of defects and the techniques that the operator can use to detect each one. The other list, called "Sample List for Selecting Proper Parts to Assemble," gives names of parts used in making the Selectric and techniques that the operator can use to identify wrong parts.

SESSION 4

In Session 4, each student continues (and culminates) his full-scale investigation of his own job by filling out the Workmanship Solution Chart. See Figure 5 at the end of this chapter. A well-thought-out solution to a workmanship problem stems from the analytical techniques developed through previous charts.

After completing that central objective of the session, the class sees a movie, *A Day in the Life of a Customer Engineer;* gets more exposure to the technical matters of tolerances, dimensioning, checking, and gauging; and is briefed on the IBM Office Products warranty and maintenance agreements.

SESSION 5

This session opens with a presentation on purchasing and its relation to quality. This is followed by a series of self-administered skill tests which involve the students very actively. A series of mechanical and electromechanical tests, representing a cross section of skills in our plant, measures each person's ability in making a timing adjustment, a clearance adjustment, linear and angular measurements, and so forth. These tests help a production person judge his manipulative skill level against that of other people. They also sometimes jar assembly people or machine-shop people into a new mutual respect for the problems and complexities faced by the other group.

The most important part of the session is devoted to each person completing the planning of his own job improvement. By this time, each student should have written a new operation description for his job and practiced it. Ideally the quality of his workmanship will have improved, after his having systematically analyzed his old ways of working and consciously developed better ways.

The very valuable results of Workmanship Analysis training can perhaps be seen more vividly through isolated examples of increased alertness than through overall, plantwide progress in quality. For example, the class period devoted to defective parts dealt with conditions of materials—their softnesses, hardnesses, and so on. This alerted a woman assembler who one day told her manager, "These fulcrum wires don't feel right. They're sort of mushy." Upon checking, it was discovered that a vendor had shipped a batch of ten or fifteen thousand wires that had not been properly heat-treated. If that defect had not been detected, a great number of our typewriters might have developed serious problems in four to six months. The woman was given a special recognition award of $500.

A stock handler, not ordinarily expected to know anything about plating, was putting parts away in a stockroom when, having been alerted by his classroom training, he decided that certain parts didn't look right. Checking them against previous stock, he observed that their sheen was a little different. Again, a vendor had shipped parts that had not been properly plated. It was a functional part that could result in trouble at a later time. Again, a special award was given for vigilance about quality.

Not long ago, we worked on a special order of a number of machines for a customer needing a special motor. An expediter—a nontechnical man not expected to know the innards of a typewriter—noticed that certain lead wires looked different from those he had seen at a meeting on this particular order. His watchfulness saved us the embarrassment of shipping a special order which did not meet the specifications. Again, an award.

Regarding awards, a product manager could authorize a special recognition award up to $500; the plant management committee (composed of the nine top plant executives), up to $1,500; the vice president for manufacturing, up to $5,000. Special awards may go as high as $10,000 when approved by division headquarters.

People must be constantly assured that someone who makes an important contribution gets something out of it for himself. Awards should be announced on bulletin boards and at department meetings. The cash is important, but so is the recognition. A most important form of recognition is the action that is taken as a result of someone's suggestion or vigilance. That action should be taken as visibly as possible.

As for the overall results of Workmanship Analysis training, they have already been cited in the Introduction: Out-of-box problems were reduced from a level of more than 25 percent to less than 10 percent. Hours put into warranty service have been cut by more than half.

The unexpected thing is that after the Workmanship

Analysis program was completed we also detected an improvement in efficiency, although that was not a goal of the course. The best explanation we can make of it is that improved work at the subassembly level led to less time for rework and adjustment during final assembly. Every program we have undertaken has produced side pluses, sometimes small, sometimes large, that we did not anticipate. I have concluded that a good program—one that meets its objective—can be expected to meet a few unexpected objectives that were never even set.

That is why some kind of program should be going on all the time. Last year's achievements should never be good enough for next year. That puts people to sleep, when they really want and need new challenges, new ways to test themselves. But more about that in Chapter 11, on goals.

Figure 3. Workmanship conditions chart.

INSTRUCTIONS: Make out this chart whenever you have bad conditions to report. Read each question carefully, and CHECK (√) the appropriate answer — YES or NO. Turn in to your manager.

YOUR NAME *Johnson, S.*		DATE *21 Sept. 65*
11 9 DEPT. NO.	MACH. GR.	PART OR ASSEMBLY
Selectric 723-725 Sp. Retaining clip		
PART NAME, PROCEDURE, JOB OR MODEL NO.		
435-438 OPER. NO.	*2nd Stage adjusting* OPERATION DESCRIPTION	

	YES	NO
WORK INSTRUCTIONS		
1. Do you have a definite job or work assignment?	√	
2. Do you understand exactly what you are to do?	√	
3. Are written instructions or job breakdowns up to date and available?		√
4. Have you been thoroughly instructed (trained) in how to do your work?		√
5. Do you perform the operations in the same sequence as stated in the instructions or job breakdown(s)?		√
6. Do you understand the effects and relationships of the operations that occur just before and after your own job operations?		√
7. Do you know what your work contributes to the use or purpose of the finished product?	√	
8. Do you agree with the instructions?		√
WORK STATION ENVIRONMENT		
9. Is your work station neat and well-organized to the best advantage for doing the work?	√	
10. Do surrounding conditions provide a good environment for the accomplishment of your work?	√	
11. Have work simplification and job improvement methods been applied to your work station?	√	
TOOLS AND EQUIPMENT		
12. Do you have proper and adequate tools and equipment for doing quality work?	√	
13. Do you know how to use all tools, jigs, fixtures, and equipment provided to help you achieve quality work?	√	
14. Are special tools and equipment for which you have occasional use accessible and readily available?	√	
MATERIALS AND PARTS		
15. Are materials, parts, components, etc., received by you in proper containers and adequate supply?		√
16. Are materials, parts, components, etc., of good quality when received by you?		√

(Figure 3 continued)

		YES	NO
17.	Do you know the procedure for notifying management and staff of off-specification or bad parts?	✓	___

TEST EQUIPMENT AND INSPECTION

18.	Do you have the proper gauges and instruments for checking and testing your work? Are they recently calibrated?	✓	___
19.	Do you know how to use the gauges, instruments, etc., provided for checking and testing your work?	✓	___
20.	Do you regularly make all tests called for in your job or work instructions?	✓	___
21.	By checking your own work closely, can you guarantee its quality in the end product?	✓	___

CHANGES

22.	Are you properly informed when engineering or manufacturing changes are made affecting your work?	✓	___
23.	Have you made any suggestions for the improvement of your work, work station, the process, or the product during the last year?	✓	___

WHAT, IN YOUR JUDGMENT, IS THE <u>WORST CONDITION</u> AFFECTING YOUR WORK? *Missing and/or broken parts shipped down (clip-retaining) the line from other operators — Rechecking and adjusting if necessary other operators' operations. — One particular operation that could and should be set during assembly in another area (line lock bracket).*

In the space below, please provide any particular additional information that you think will help describe the conditions checked "No."

QUESTION NUMBER	EXPLANATION OR DISCUSSION
3	*New parts and procedure not on instructions.*
5, 6	*I think my way is faster. Never worked on jobs prior or behind me.*
15	*Improper containers and supply is inadequate at times.*
16	*Parts are often mixed and broken.*

Wherever there are checks in the "No" column, describe each such condition in more detail on the Workmanship Analysis Chart.

_____	*21 Sept. 65*	*S. Johnson*
MANAGER'S SIGNATURE	DATE	EMPLOYEE'S SIGNATURE

Figure 4. Workmanship analysis chart.

STATE BRIEFLY THE WORKMANSHIP <u>CONDITION</u> THAT YOU ARE ANALYZING:	YOUR NAME *Johnson, S.*	DATE *22 Sept. 65*

STATE BRIEFLY THE WORKMANSHIP <u>CONDITION</u>
THAT YOU ARE ANALYZING:
Number 23 - Missing and/or broken
parts shipped down the line from
other operations and in a great
many cases the parts are assembled
where they will have to be repositioned.

YOUR NAME *Johnson, S.*   DATE *22 Sept. 65*
119
DEPT. NO.   MACH. GR.   PART NO. OR ASSEMBLY
Selectric 723-725 - Spring Retaining   *Clip*
PART NAME, PROCEDURE, JOB OR MODEL NO.
435-438   *2nd Stage Adjusting*
OPER. NO.   OPERATION DESCRIPTION

INSTRUCTIONS: CHECK (√) EVERY ITEM THAT APPLIES. CHECK (√) AND WRITE IN "OTHER" ITEMS THAT YOU BELIEVE ARE IMPORTANT.

1. FROM WHAT SOURCE WAS THIS PROBLEM CONDITION FIRST REPORTED? (CHECK √)

    √ DISCOVERED BY OPERATOR
    ___ WORKMANSHIP CONDITION REPORT
    ___ PRODUCT TEST REPORT
    ___ QUALITY ENGINEERING AUDIT

    ___ "W.A.R." REPORT
    ___ FIELD REPORT
    ___ RELIABILITY & SERVICEABILITY REPORT
    ___ OTHER_____

2. IF THE PROBLEM SITUATION IS CONNECTED WITH LACK OF INFORMATION, CHECK (√) AREA WHERE INFORMATION IS LACKING.

    ___ JOB ASSIGNMENT
    ___ WORK PROCESS; ROUTINGS
    ___ JOB INSTRUCTIONS AND JOB TRAINING
    ___ ENGINEERING SPECIFICATIONS
    ___ JOB OPERATIONS
    ___ WORK STATION
    ___ WORKING CONDITIONS
    ___ WORKMANSHIP CHECKING TECHNIQUES

    ___ PARTS; COMPONENTS; MATERIALS
    ___ TOOLS; EQUIPMENT
    ___ GAUGES; INSPECTION INSTRUMENTS
    ___ WORK PERFORMANCE RECORD
    ___ PRODUCTION LEVEL
    ___ QUALITY REQUIREMENTS
    ___ REJECTED WORK
    √ OTHER: *Not taking time to position*
    ___ UNKNOWN *part correctly so it wouldn't have to be repositioned*

3. FROM WHICH OF THE FOLLOWING AREAS DOES THE PROBLEM CONDITION SEEM TO ARISE? (CHECK √)

    ___ DESIGNING
    ___ ENGINEERING (PRODUCT; MANUFACTURING)
    ___ MACHINING
    ___ METAL FORMING
    ___ METAL TREATMENT (PLATE, HEAT TREAT, PAINT, MECHANICAL FINISH)
    √ ASSEMBLY

    ___ SUPPLIES MANUFACTURING
    ___ SHIPPING
    ___ PURCHASING – VENDOR
    ___ TESTING
    ___ PACKING
    ___ OTHER_____
    ___ UNKNOWN

4. WHICH OF THE FOLLOWING FACTORS SEEMS TO BE CONTRIBUTING TO THE PROBLEM CONDITION? (CHECK √)

    ___ ADJUSTING - TIMING
    ___ ADJUSTING - MOTION
    ___ ADJUSTING - CLEARANCE
    ___ ALIGNMENT
    ___ BENT PARTS; KINKS
    ___ OFF-SPEC PARTS
    ___ FASTENERS (SCREWS, C-CLIPS, RETAINERS, ADHESIVES, ETC.)
    ___ SURFACE ROUGHNESS
    ___ FRICTION
    ___ LUBRICATION
    ___ HARDNESS-SOFTNESS; HEAT TREAT

    ___ RUST-CORROSION; PLATING
    ___ TENSION-COMPRESSION: PRESSURE
    ___ TWISTING; SHEAR
    ___ CONDUCTION - INSULATION
    ___ CIRCUIT SITUATIONS
    √ MOVEMENT; HANDLING METHODS
    ___ EXPANSION-CONTRACTION
    ___ SURFACE CONDITION; PAINT
    √ OTHER *Simply left off*
    ___ OTHER_____
    ___ UNKNOWN

    ENVIRONMENTAL FACTORS:
    ___ LAYOUT-SPACE
    ___ NOISE; SOUND
    ___ DRAFTS
    ___ MOISTURE
    ___ LIGHT; GLARE
    ___ VIBRATION
    ___ HEAT-COLD
    ___ DUST; DIRT; FOREIGN MATTER
    ___ OTHER_____
    ___ OTHER_____
    ___ OTHER_____
    √ UNKNOWN

5. WHO WILL HAVE TO ACT TO ELIMINATE OR CORRECT THE PROBLEM CONDITION? (CHECK √)

    √ SELF
    √ OTHER EMPLOYEE
    √ MANAGER
    ___ PROJECT MANAGER

    ___ STAFF
    ___ TESTER OR INSPECTOR
    ___ REPAIRMAN
    ___ OTHERS: (STATE)_____
    ___ UNKNOWN_____

(Figure 4 continued)

6. WHAT ACTIONS COULD BE TAKEN TO CORRECT THE PROBLEM SITUATION? (CHECK √)

____ CAN ANYTHING BE COMBINED OR SEPARATED	√ CAN ANYTHING BE ELIMINATED
____ CAN PLACE BE MODIFIED OR CHANGED	____ CAN PERSON BE CHANGED
____ CAN TIME OR SEQUENCE BE MODIFIED OR CHANGED .	____ CAN ANYTHING BE IMPROVED
	____ OTHER ACTION _____
	____ UNKNOWN

7. LIST BRIEFLY THE SPECIFIC SOURCES, CAUSES, OR REASONS FOR THE PROBLEM CONDITION, BASED ON THIS ANALYSIS. *The specific part is a spring clip - it could come off during handling, could be left off by operator, or could be assembled so it would fly off with just a small jolt.*

1 — when assembled in the wrong position it is absolutely necessary that it be repositioned because it governs the amount of tension to be placed on a particular spring.

8. MAKE A DIAGRAM OR SKETCH, OR ANY OTHER EXPLANATION, WHICH WILL ADD TO A BETTER UNDER-STANDING OF THE PROBLEM SITUATION AND CONDITIONS.

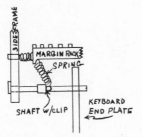

NEXT STEP: BY USING THE <u>WORKMANSHIP SOLUTION CHART</u> TO SOLVE THE PROBLEM YOU MAY QUALIFY FOR A SUGGESTION AWARD.

_____	_____	*S. Johnson*	*22 Sept. 65*
MANAGER'S SIGNATURE	DATE	EMPLOYEE'S SIGNATURE	DATE

Figure 5. Workmanship solution chart.

1. WHAT IS THE <u>PROBLEM</u>? *Missing -
Broken - and mal-posi-
tioning of parts*

Johnson, S.		24 Sept. 65
YOUR NAME		DATE
119		
DEPT. NO.	MACH. GR.	PART OR ASSEMBLY
Spring Retaining Clip - 723-725 Lil.		
PART NAME, PROCEDURE, JOB OR MODEL NO.		
435-438	*2nd Stage adjusting*	
OPER. NO.	OPERATION DESCRIPTION	

2. LIST ACTUAL CONDITIONS AND OTHER INFORMATION:

*Eliminate waste of time to operator - when
replacing and/or repositioning the retaining
clip*

3. WHAT ARE THE DESIRED CONDITIONS OR OBJECTIVES OF A SUCCESSFUL SOLUTION?

*For the part to be intact and positioned correctly
so future operators will not have to spend
time readjusting to get the desired results.*

4. IF KNOWN, DESCRIBE THE MOST LIKELY CAUSE OF THE PROBLEM:

① *Handling machines in reckless manner*
② *Inadequate tension on spring to hold position*
③ *Assembly methods careless (operator not
positioning part correctly to start with)*

5. LIST THE POSSIBLE SOLUTIONS OR CORRECTIONS TO THE PROBLEM:

1. *Devise a more adequate means of insuring
correct positioning of part.*
2. *Eliminate part by redesigning shaft on
which clip is affixed.*

(Figure 5 continued)

6. WHAT IS THE SOLUTION THAT YOU RECOMMEND?

I ___ I recommend the shaft be redesigned to
eliminate the spring retaining clip.

II ___ Alternative - Redesign the retaining clip
applicator.

7. DESCRIBE HOW THE SOLUTION SHOULD BE PUT INTO EFFECT. USE ADDITIONAL SHEETS IF NECESSARY.

I ___ The solution I have in mind would be to
score the shaft on which the retaining clip is
now used [the retaining clip is used to hold
tension on the margin rack (rebound tension)].
Do away with clip. Tension spring could
be held in position now by the groove in
the shaft. This would eliminate the first
operation of installing the part.

II ___ Redesign clip applicator so it will correctly
place clip in same position every time.

clip holder → clip

Extension affixed
to Tool to assure
proper positioning
of retaining clip.

End View
Present Tool

Side View
Redesigned Tool

_____   _____   S. Johnson   21 Sept. 65
MANAGER'S SIGNATURE   DATE   EMPLOYEE'S SIGNATURE   DATE

HAVE I SUBMITTED A SUGGESTION?   Yes

7

TOTAL RESPONSIBILITY
THE ENEMY OF BOREDOM

Not long ago a writer for *Fortune* coined a phrase that has preoccupied the pages of magazines and has been the subject of industrial conferences around the world and of any number of worried conversations in boardrooms and private dining rooms. The phrase is "blue collar blues."

The phrase symbolizes a syndrome of industrial ills that are well known: high absenteeism, especially on Mondays and Fridays; excessive employee turnover; widespread employee indifference to quality; the disdain that some young employees appear to feel for routine, repetitive work, which many managers relate to the rising education level of young people; surliness of some production people toward their foremen and managers; occasional wildcat stoppages, even sabotage of production; and perhaps most alarming of all, growing evidence that the disaffection, usually blamed on the young, is shared by older employees as well.

Industry has become rightly alarmed. The illness threatens the continued manufacturing leadership of the United States and other leading industrial nations. Yet how is this threat most often discussed? It is usually reduced down to a simple—perhaps too simple—question: "What are we going to do about *boredom?*"

And the answer, at least in almost every article and conversation I've come across, is furnished by another catchy phrase: "job enrichment."

Both the diagnosis (boredom) and the cure (job enrichment) are neat and satisfying. At least they are labels, and we always seem to feel better when we can attach a label to something. But under scrutiny, these particular labels leave us empty-handed. I, for one, find them inadequate as a basis for action.

Let's take boredom first. Production work is often boring, true. So are most management duties: preparing reports, attending dull meetings, exercising patience. So are many duties of the home which, even in this day of liberation, many women wouldn't think of giving up: preparing meals, making beds, tending to children. So are many activities that "bored" production workers eagerly choose to do in their leisure time: fishing, mowing the lawn, painting the house. The simple fact is that human beings have enormous capacity to endure boredom and repetition—if they can personally identify with the *purpose* of the boredom. A man mows his lawn a dozen times a summer (what could be more boring?) because his name is on the letterbox out front, because he is proud of his piece of land. A politician sits through interminable chicken-and-peas dinners because his name will be

on the voting machine come November. A woodworking
hobbyist sandpapers a piece of lumber into a satiny surface—
boring, repetitious—while anticipating his pride at showing
his friends the coffee table he made. Think of the boredom
of an archeologist sifting through rubble in search of his
prize; of a scholar in a library searching for an elusive fact;
of a dentist drilling tooth after tooth. We all gladly endure
boredom if our tasks are wrapped in personal or small-group
identity. Boredom is not the issue. Personal identity is.

And how about "job enrichment" as the cure? What does
it mean? In one company it means rotation of duties to avoid
boredom. In another it means enlargement of duties—just
adding tasks. In still another, it may mean giving workers
some say about their working conditions. All these may be
commendable, but they don't add up to strong personal
identification with one's work. When I hear the term "job
enrichment," I can't help but visualize some manager going
down the assembly line spooning out vitamins, as though jobs
were baby food. Can you imagine an assembler announcing
proudly to his wife and kids over the supper table, "I had
my job enriched today"?

But there's another statement that any breadwinner would
proudly tell his family, whether he's a vice president, a
first-line manager, a sales engineer—or an assembler. Any
human being feels bigger and better for being able to say,
"Today, my boss put me in full charge of my job. He gave
me total responsibility."

There is no substitute for responsibility. Responsibility
does not mean merely more tasks to do. It does not mean
more pleasant surroundings for doing them. It does not
mean more variety. It means giving a person *charge* of what
he does. It means holding him, and him alone, accountable
for his work; no passing the buck to an inspector. It means
the person knows how his work fits into the total job—and
he knows that others know it. Thus all his co-workers, each
identifiably responsible for their part of the total job, rely

on him. He will be respected for doing his work well and blamed for doing it poorly. Human beings thrive on personal and small-group responsibility.

On an athletic team, that kind of personal responsibility is essential. In any well-organized management, that is how responsibility is delegated. Manufacturing will reach its full maturity in human terms—and in efficiency—when every person engaged in it, down to the participant with the least sophisticated assignment, is held totally responsible for his performance.

The problem is not boredom, but depersonalization. The answer is not "enrichment," but direct experience of personal worth and importance, of social responsibility that derives from clearly defined *personal* responsibility.

The overarching theme of everything we've done in manufacturing IBM office products is *total responsibility*, bottom to top, top to bottom, wall to wall. While we have not fully achieved it, and perhaps never will, it is our constant aim. Every program described earlier in this book—merit pay, merit promotion, full employment, work simplification, and workmanship analysis—flows toward this goal, and every chapter that follows is an extension of it. This discussion on total responsibility will occupy four chapters.

Having thus warned the reader of the elaborate emphasis I am about to place on it, let me now confess that I got my first "course" in total responsibility under the tutelage of a janitor.

One night in our old New York State plant, shortly before we moved to Lexington, I was in my office a little late when a man came in to see me. He was a member of our 40-man crew that cleaned the plant during the second shift. He was nervous and obviously unhappy; I asked what was on his mind. He replied, "I never get to clean the toilets." Well, that was one complaint I'd never expected to hear. He amplified his complaint and came up with a proposition that wasn't as crazy as it first seemed: "Look, all I do is sweep the floor. Nobody ever notices if the floor is really clean when the rest of the place is dirty. Would you let me have one section of this plant, one-fortieth of it, and let me sweep the floor, clean the desks, dump the wastepaper baskets, clean the toilets, do everything there is to do? Just let it be my section. Then all I'll ask is that you look at my section every morning and compare it to someone else's section. I think I can do the best job on the crew, and I want to prove it.''

That man was asking to *redesign his job*—and in a particular and sophisticated way. Translated into the higher-flown terms of management, he was telling me that his job was designed horizonally—by function—rather than vertically—by responsibility. The fact is that most jobs in industry, management as well as production, are designed horizontally, by function. This janitor was saying that the horizontal approach, always thought to be more efficient, is fundamentally inefficient because it destroys personal identification and motivation. And I absolutely agree with him.

What that man wanted was total responsibility. He realized that the job he wanted was a relatively small part of the larger job of cleaning the plant, which in turn was part of the larger job of *operating* the plant. But this janitor-theoretician believed, as I do, that every job no matter how broad (plant manager) or how fine (janitor) ought to be so designed that the person doing it is *accountable*, clearly and unambiguously, for performance. That is a simple but powerful idea.

While dissatisfied, he was not complaining about boredom. "Enriching" his duties by adding variety for its own sake— one hour of sweeping, another of toilet cleaning—would not have given him satisfaction. He wanted *responsibility*, a vertically organized job with his name on it. He was so eager to win credit for good work that he was willing to risk discredit for poor work.

That suggests a vital principle of job organization. The

organization

principle applies from the highest management job down to
the lowest production or service rank: *When something goes
wrong and you don't know whose fault it is, the project is
badly organized.*

Sure, when something goes wrong, one can always say
that the manager in charge is responsible. But that's not
the way it works in real life. Until a short while ago, every
time I visited our assembly plant in Bogotá I heard complaints that parts received from Lexington had arrived
dented and damaged. I couldn't believe it. I knew that our
shipping people were careful packers. Finally one day a
couple of us went to shipping, intercepted a box about to
be shipped to Bogotá, and opened it. It was filled with
carefully packed containers—except that someone had loosely
dumped a few dozen parts into the space at the top. I told
the shipping manager in charge that this was intolerable. I
instructed him to identify the man who had done it and
fire him; that man didn't belong in our business.

Three or four days later, the manager called me to say
he couldn't identify the individual because four or five people
had filled those boxes. There was just no way of knowing
who had done the dumping. From that day on, the "janitor
principle" was invoked in the shipping department. I told
the manager, "One person is to be responsible for that
Bogotá box—and every other box that goes out of here. No
more of this business of five people doing it and two people
inspecting it. Next time it happens, if you don't know who
to fire, *you've* got to go." That was the end of the trouble.

To conclude about my friend the janitor, if we hadn't
been about to move to Lexington, we would have given that
man his own piece of the plant to clean. In fact, we would
have turned his idea into a bit of cost-cutting. We would
have divided the plant into 30 or 35 sections, rather than 40,
raised the responsibility level of the job, and increased the
salary accordingly. My guess is that having a smaller cleaning
crew, with each person totally responsible for his work,

would have given us a cleaner plant—and given the janitors more satisfaction in accomplishing it.

In Lexington we subcontract our cleaning work—but I've never forgotten my "tutor." His approach has spread through everything we do.

Redesigning jobs for total responsibility is a long, difficult, meticulous business. Unless the goal is clearly understood, the process can easily go wrong. It is very tempting to redesign jobs just for the sake of change, adding variety under the illusion of giving true responsibility.

The best way I know to fix in mind the idea of true responsibility is to listen to the voices of those who don't have it—and who crave it. Magazines, books, and television documentaries, caught up by the chant of the "blue collar blues," have been quoting people in blue collars and white collars, open collars and necktied collars, about their dissatis-factions. For months I have been collecting these quotations, but have been reading them with different spectacles than those of most analysts When read through the lenses of "job boredom," these quotations make a case for boredom. But when read through the lenses of total responsibility, these statements make a stronger case for ambition, for the simple desire of every person to be recognized—and held accountable for what he does.

Cal S., 26, has worked for the past four years in Los Angeles, lifting heavy cases of swimming-pool-cleaning acid from a conveyor and shoving them toward a truck-loading dock. *Newsweek* magazine recently quoted him on his bore-dom, but I read another message. The quotation: "You're on a half hour and you're off a half hour. That's four hours of real physical labor. The other time you're looking for leakers. The job is *very* monotonous. Being a peon, I don't have any say in the company. The waste bothers me, but I'm in a situation where I can't say anything." [1]

In the same article, *Newsweek* also reported the comments of some white collar workers. Sandy C., a 23-year-old secretary to two lawyers in one of Chicago's largest law firms, says she "just feels like a machine." Each morning some 50 secretaries on her floor "come in like a thundering herd. My father always told me that when you're working and making money, you're happy. But it's not as simple as that. To be happy, you have to feel that you're making some sort of contribution. And that's difficult when you have a supervisor staring at you every minute like you're going to do something wrong."

Another young woman of higher rank and salary, Deanne R., 25, an executive secretary in Atlanta, feels trapped by her $10,000 salary, complaining that she has never really been challenged. "After six months, you've got the system down. . . . I begin to analyze my job too much, question whether I'm really *making any impact*. I can't get another job in what I'm doing because I'm overpriced. The company makes you put up with all the crap by paying you well." [2]

Mike F., late 30s, a laborer in a steel mill, is quoted by Studs Terkel in a new book on work: "I feel like the guys who built the pyramids. Somebody built 'em. Somebody built the Empire State Building, too. There's hard work behind it. I would like to see a building, say the Empire State, with a foot-wide strip from top to bottom, and the name of every bricklayer on it, the name of every electrician. So when a guy walked by, he could take his son and say: 'See, that's me over there on the 45th floor. I put that steel beam in.' Picasso can point to a painting. I think I've done harder work than Picasso and what can I point to? Everybody should have something to point to." [3]

Are these frustrations borne only by those in the obscurity of the big office or factory? Consider Terkel's interview with 37-year-old Steve H., who had just ended a career he'd dreamed of as a boy, as a major league baseball pitcher. This man stated the same yearning for recognition: "I've never been a big star. I've done about as good as I can with the equipment I have. I played with Mickey Mantle and Willie

Mays. People always recognize them. But for someone to recognize me, it really made me feel good. I think everybody gets a kick out of feeling special."

In contrast, take a couple of people whose work is routine as can be, yet who derive immense satisfaction because their "job design" enables them to take personal pride in doing it well. A waitress, Yolanda L.: "When I put the plate down, you don't hear a sound. When I pick up a glass, I want it to be just right. When someone says, 'How come you're just a waitress?' I say, 'Don't you think you deserve being served by me?'" Paul D. feels personal responsibility in hauling steel on an interstate truck: "Every load is a challenge. I have problems in the morning with heartburn. I can't eat. Once I off-load, the pressure is gone. Then I can eat anything. I accomplished something." [4]

The Saab motorcar people of Sweden have recently shifted to making jobs more satisfying by making their people more responsible. They have gone further than that. Sensing the sales appeal of a car made by workers with personal responsibility, Saab has been selling the point in their product ads:

> *Bored people build bad cars. That's why we're doing away with the assembly line.*
>
> Working on an assembly line is monotonous. And boring. And after a while, some people begin not to care about their jobs anymore. So the quality of the product often suffers.
>
> That's why, at Saab, we're replacing the assembly line with assembly teams. Groups of just three or four people who are responsible for a particular assembly process from start to finish. . . . The result: People are more involved. They care more. So there's less absenteeism, less turnover. And we have more experienced people on the job. . . .

Whether in factory or office, whether in management or lower ranks, wherever one sees successful attacks on job "boredom," the solutions, often misnamed "enrichment," are really downward delegations of specific and total responsibility. *The Wall Street Journal* recently published a long, first-page story titled: "Boredom Fighters Put Variety in Many Jobs, Find Productivity Rises."

This headline, like almost all analyses of the problem, missed the point. The problem described in the article has little to do with boredom; the successes cited have even less to do with variety. The story starts right off with an anecdote in which no responsibility changes to total responsibility:

> NEW YORK—Ada Traynham well remembers her old job at Chemical Bank here. Even a machine would have grown bored with it. "My job was to pull invoices and checks out of envelopes and stack them into three piles: one under $10, another between $10 and $25 and a third over $25. Then I'd pass the piles on to the next person," she recalls. "After two months of this, I was so bored I would have quit within another month."
>
> That was about two years ago, and the young clerk is still with Chemical. But instead of performing a tiny task in the paperwork mill, she now handles all the processing for 22 corporate accounts, from crediting payments to returning unsigned checks. "Handling your own accounts is a lot more interesting, and you feel like you've accomplished something," she says. "What you do is what the customer gets." [5]

In the four years prior to the change, turnover in Mrs. Traynham's department averaged a staggering 59 percent a year. It has since been slashed to 24 percent, in line with the bank's overall rate. Pushing responsibility downward, of course, upheaves a manager's concept of his job. In many places this leads to fear and resistance by managers at all levels, which dissipates only after the manager is convinced he is now free to do a bigger job better.

At Chemical Bank, Raymond Farrell, an assistant treasurer in charge of 185 employees, told *The Wall Street Journal*: "In the past, this job was a simple operation—just get out there and bark, put out the fires, get the work done and don't rock the boat." But now, he says, "thirty-five to forty percent of what used to come to this desk no longer does. Previously I thought I knew all there was to know about this operation. Now I can't see myself learning it all even years from now," he says, adding that he is free to concentrate on creative new approaches to cutting unit labor costs and boosting productivity.

The *Wall Street Journal* article also described downward delegation—with total responsibility—at the brokerage firm of Merrill Lynch, Pierce, Fenner & Smith:

> . . . "A year or so ago, I was sometimes spending four hours a day on the telephone answering questions from brokers," says William Van Vorst, a clerical supervisor at Merrill Lynch. The processing of stock certificates in his office was so broken down into tiny tasks that only the supervisor could handle a question about the end result, he says.
>
> But today, each clerk handles all of the office's work on a certificate and takes responsibility for it. When she rejects an improperly prepared certificate, she signs her name and telephone extension to the paperwork and handles any calls from the brokers.
>
> "This has cut 70% of my phone calls," says Mr. Van Vorst. "Now, for the first time, I really have time for planning," he says. Among other things, he now is planning how the office can add an additional function without increasing the number of workers. At the same time, having responsibility for a complete unit of work has given the clerks a chance to obtain "feedback" on how well they are doing on their jobs, Mr. Van Vorst says. This has boosted productivity and cut the error rate, he adds.

Reading through the rising mountain of literature on this subject, we get a picture of managers worried about losing bored and restless employees. But company presidents and directors had better start worrying about losing bored and restless *managers*. What are managers restless about? Insufficient responsibility. Harold Rush, a senior specialist at The Conference Board, observes, "Companies often say, 'You're responsible—but you can't spend over $1,000 on your own.' " [6]

A 1972 survey by the American Management Associations [7] showed that among middle managers—traditionally a loyal group of "company believers"—74 percent thought frustration and discontent were on the rise. Among middle managers under 30, the figure rose to 83 percent. The AMA report stated: "Today's manager reports that his opportunities for direct participation in the decision-making process seem to be rapidly decreasing in the highly bureaucratic and authoritarian structure of the techno-corporation of the 1970s. Moreover, the sense of challenge and the feelings of personal reward and personal achievement seem to be diminishing. . . ."

Roy H. Walters, a New Jersey management consultant, is one of the pioneer users of the term "job enrichment." Yet even he makes a sharp distinction between what many consider "enrichment" and the more direct approach of conferring real responsibility. Conceding that such niceties as better lighting and bowling clubs may be commendable for their own sake, he points out that these don't get full results because they deal only with the fringes of the work experience: "Managers say, 'I don't understand why the employees don't perform better; we treat them so well.' Sure, we've spent billions of dollars to treat people better. But people don't want to be treated better; they want to be used better."[8]

References

1. *Newsweek,* "The Job Blahs: Who Wants to Work?" March 26, 1973.
2. Ibid.
3. Studs Terkel, *Working.* New York: Pantheon Books, 1974.
4. Ibid.
5. Roger Rickleff, "Boredom Fighters Put Variety in Many Jobs, Find Productivity Rises," *The Wall Street Journal,* August 21, 1972. Reprinted with the permission of The Wall Street Journal, © Dow Jones & Company, Inc., 1972.
6. Ibid.
7. Alfred T. DeMaria, Dale Tarnowieski, and Richard Gurman, "Manager Unions?" AMA Research Report. AMACOM, 1972.
8. *The Wall Street Journal,* op. cit.

HOW TO INSTALL
TOTAL RESPONSIBILITY

Every man or woman in industry, whether placed high or low, at some time has personally experienced the humiliation of having his or her best judgment trampled upon thoughtlessly. That is a morale killer. Worse than that, it serves notice on the victim not to risk offering his best judgment again.

An example from my own observation that always comes to mind occurred shortly after World War II when I was working for a project manager who also had under him a group of tool designers, skilled and diligent men who might devote a month to perfecting the design of a single tool. This project manager insisted on scrutinizing every design before it was sent out to a vendor for price quotations. Okay, that wasn't too bad; perhaps it was his way of exercising "responsibility." But he had a maddening habit. Before even looking at the design, he'd open the drawer of his desk and pull out a red pencil. While the designer—who had toiled for a month over that piece of paper—stood there, the manager would start slashing away with a red mark here, a change there, all in a few minutes, then hand it back and say, "Okay, now it's ready to send out for quotes." The furious designer would charge by my desk muttering, "I hope the damned thing doesn't work!"

Often the tool *didn't* work. And who was responsible when it didn't? The designer whose work had been mutilated, or the project manager who had distorted the design? How much wiser that project manager would have been to have examined the drawings carefully—with no red pencil—asking a question here or there, giving the designer an opportunity to support his rationale, getting the designer's reaction to ideas for improvement, and then saying, "Let's try it." Better still, why didn't he make a policy of not looking at the drawings at all, but respecting the skill of his men by *assuming* their work was good, and keeping a record of whose tools worked well and whose didn't? Then, if Bill or Joe built a record of unsatisfactory designs, the manager could show the record and warn Bill or Joe to shape up. That would be a simple example of total responsibility.

Another example that keeps running through my mind comes not from manufacturing but from a great deal of travel. It's a good illustration of how the "lowliest" of jobs can be redesigned for total responsibility—for the benefit of the individual's growth, and, in turn, the organization's improvement.

Every day, every occupied hotel room is visited by a chambermaid who cleans up, changes the towels, and so on. If a faucet drips, that's not her business. If the TV set focuses poorly, that's for the house engineer to worry about (but the engineer doesn't know the set doesn't work unless an annoyed guest complains, which few do, so the next guest is also annoyed). How is the chief housekeeper, the maid's "end-of-line inspector," to know that a light bulb doesn't work, that a tub stopper is missing, that the thermostat is out of whack? She just takes a moment to check that the maid has been there and has cleaned up. *Who is in charge of the room?* Nobody. This simple responsibility is sliced up into functions—and the real responsibility falls between the cracks. That is why some of the world's largest and most expensive hotels leave their guests feeling cheated—and why an inexpensive, family-run motel often makes a guest feel he's visited someone's well-kept home.

If the manager of a large hotel or motel were to adopt the IBM Office Products approach to total responsibility, here's how he would do it: He would assign a chambermaid permanently to a wing or group of rooms; no switching her around from day to day. She would be *totally in charge* of those rooms—in effect acting manager of a small hotel. She would be accountable to her top manager for any customer complaints about plumbing that doesn't work, a TV set that won't tune, curtains that won't pull, beds that sag. When she calls the plumber and he doesn't come, *she* should complain to her manager, because her neck is on the line.

One of our major international motel chains indulges in the expensive practice of selling off their beds and mattresses every two years for next to nothing, replacing them with new ones, on the theory that because *some* beds wear out in two years *all* ought to be replaced. This seems a wasteful practice. Why not give a well-trained chambermaid responsibility for constant inspection of the furniture, rugs, curtains, wallpaper, and paint, letting her choose—or, at least, recommend—which ought to be replaced and which need not be? She might even be given an annual budget. Front desk clerks would be charged with keeping records of complaints and compliments, which a manager could then evaluate. If Mabel's rooms keep getting consistent compliments and Susan's get more than their fair share of complaints, the manager knows where his problem is. By delegating total responsibility downward, that manager, if he chooses and trains his people well, is assured of an ever improving hotel.

That approach, in terms familiar to every traveler, sums up what we mean by redesigning jobs for total responsibility.

In manufacturing, how is this approach applied? It requires scrutinizing—and perhaps redesigning—each job to maximize personal responsibility in line with the following questions:

1. Forget about what the person does now. What is the *job* that needs doing? (The chambermaid now makes beds and cleans; the job that needs doing is keeping the room shipshape for guests.)

2. Is that job that needs doing too much for one person? If so, how can it be divided up or reorganized so that each person remains fully accountable for the smaller job? If the job is too small for one person, what other jobs with full accountability can be added to it?

3. Is the job designed in such a way that the person automatically knows if his work is good or poor? Do his co-workers automatically know? If poor work slips through, can blame clearly be traced (even after the product reaches the customer, if a product is involved) to the individual responsible for it? Can credit be ascertained and acknowledged?

4. Does the person in question depend on any service by another person (such as machinery repair, replenishment of parts and supplies, inspection, record keeping, etc.) that he can do himself as part of his job? If his job is indirect, must he get approvals before acting? If so, how can he be held responsible for insuring that the service is accomplished?

5. Can the person look at the finished product and state exactly what he contributed to it?

Redesigning jobs to get the right answers to those questions is not always easy. In our early days of total responsibility, I was walking through the machine floor when the department manager pointed at someone and said, "How do you give *that* man total responsibility?" The man was buffing the carriage end-covers of the Executive typewriter. I noticed that this job was interdependent with that of another man, who plated the end-covers. Both jobs were essential if the piece were to come out with a polished chrome finish; either man could ruin the work of the other.

We decided that each man could quite easily learn the other's work. So each took total responsibility for half of the end-covers—not just for buffing or plating, but for the *total* finish on the parts. He'd spend one day buffing his batch, then the next day plating the pieces he'd buffed the day before. The other man would do the same, on alternating days. Now, instead of each person having the other to blame if work comes out poorly, they are in friendly competition to produce parts with a fine finish.

In our early days another troublesome problem was our data processing area. Survey after survey during this time showed that it was the lowest-morale operation in Lexington. When we looked into why, the answer was clear. We had two departments—split horizontally, by function. One group of people did all the analyzing; a totally different group did the programming. Nobody belonged to the whole job, and the whole job belonged to no one.

When we reorganized data processing, we still had two departments—but split vertically. Each manager and his group became totally responsible for the jobs assigned to them, from analyzing through programming to the final printouts of forms and reports. Suddenly we had no more complaints that one group was ruining the work of the other. Turnover was sharply reduced, as were complaints to the personnel department. And the two new groups began turning out more work than the two old ones had, though the number of people was the same.

Total responsibility has created a vast change in the large and complicated area of our plant where parts are stored. This area houses the stock for thousands of part numbers. Previously, when a shipment of parts arrived from a vendor, the first man (or men) available broke open the boxes, made entries on inventory cards, and put the stock away in the proper bins. Similarly, when a requisition for parts arrived from a production department, whoever happened to get the order filled it. The work was considered among the most boring in the plant. Moreover, accuracy of inventory was always a big problem. This does not mean parts disappeared; it just means that records were often incorrect. Too often, inventory of a certain part fell below the minimum reserve without anyone taking responsibility to report the shortage, sometimes resulting in costly production slowdowns. Nobody really cared, except the harried manager—and he had no way to make his *people* care.

Our total-responsibility drive changed all that. The manager divided the stockroom into sections, with one man responsible for each section and everything that happened in it: putting the stock away, accuracy of count and records, promptness in filling orders, maintaining ample stock, neatness of the area, and so forth. The old problems disappeared. Morale and interest in the job improved, and the men began competing to have the best-running, best-looking, most accurate section in the stockroom. Each man was his own manager.

On the assembly line itself, where total responsibility is most difficult to design, we are finding ways to do it. At first they were baby-step ways; our most recent giant-step ways will be described later, in the chapters on simplified business procedures. In some plants we put assemblers in charge of their own parts supplies. Why should an assembler have to make out a requisition for screws, wait for them, and then blame some unnamed soul when the screws don't arrive? Why couldn't he just get them himself? Why couldn't he keep his own records of parts-in and products-out? Why couldn't he learn to make minor repairs and adjustments of his own machinery, instead of depending on a repairman who might be busy elsewhere? Why couldn't he take charge of his own quality inspection and rework? Why did he have to go through his manager to deal with other people—the assemblers before and after him, supply and service people, anyone in other departments who affects him? Why does the assembler have to stay frozen in his workplace, with everyone coming to *him?*

Regarding the latter point, some managers might view this increased freedom as time lost from the assembler's regular job. However, the idea that any person can or will work at full efficiency on a single, probably monotonous, job day after day with never a break is not realistic. We found that once assemblers were freed to come and go, to see whoever they needed to see, to get something done, some indirect expense was eliminated, problems were solved more expeditiously, the assemblers became more valuable and responsible persons, and their job satisfaction was immensely increased.

The foregoing indicates how we have pushed—and keep pushing—to create total responsibility in *individual* jobs. A more advanced effort—our dominant one in recent years—has been assigning total responsibility for assembling the entire typewriter to *small groups*. Within these groups, individuals are given more responsibility than they were previously.

This system accomplishes two major goals. While increasing job satisfaction through enlargement of individual responsibility, it also creates a small-team responsibility for the entire product, with all the interdependencies usually associated with a team. We have found these interdependencies to be a valuable motivator.

The chief thrust of small-group responsibility within IBM, as with numerous other manufacturing companies, has been toward the shortened assembly line, or what we have come to call the *mini-line.* Simply stated, under the old "long line" way, assembling a complete typewriter from parts and subassemblies required a line of as many as 80 to 100 people, each doing a two- to three-minute task—repeatedly, repeatedly, repeatedly, all day long. The mini-line is composed of 10 to 20 people. Each person is in charge of a complex of related tasks, such as the total adjustment of a mechanism. This may mean working on a single typewriter for 10 to 18 minutes.

The line itself is shaped in such a way (we have two main shapings, to be described) that each person in the line can see every other person. Moreover, the typewriter itself, moving along the line, is always in view of every person. Thus, the first assembler on the line, who usually performs the simplest tasks, can see his work turn into a finished product at the end of the line. If someone does poor or incomplete work, he cannot escape its consequences. A co-worker a few feet away will be stuck with the trouble—and confront the person responsible for negligence. Conversely, when a perfect typewriter passes through final adjustment at the end of the line, it's a visible credit to every individual in the group.

That solution may sound simple, but it's the outgrowth of many complications and problems. Let's look at our plant in Amsterdam, Holland, where the mini-line was introduced after it was pioneered by our small plant in Sumare, Brazil (soon to be followed by Lexington, Toronto, and Berlin). Amsterdam supplies typewriters for about 75 countries, mostly in Europe, the Mideast, and Africa. As in any of our plants, these machines, each built to the individual specifications of a customer, are assembled in a bewildering variety of carriage lengths, colors, type styles, and optional features. But as supplier to so many countries, Amsterdam has the immensely greater complication of having to equip its machines with 38 different keyboards and 12 different voltage groups. Even two countries that employ essentially the same alphabets, such as England and France, require different keyboards because they use different symbols and accent marks. Some machines, such as those for Israel, must be activated in reverse so the typing progresses from right to left. Rarely are two machines identical, and each machine must proceed along the assembly line with a card specifying its exact requirements. In a sense, every typewriter is custom-made.

The long production line was invented for the repeated assembly of identical products. The variations in our product turned out to be a major source of the constant problems we had on our long production line. If a typewriter goes through 80 pairs of hands, there are 80 short delays while each operator, handling a new machine every two or three minutes, examines a card to check the specifications of his next typewriter; there are 80 chances for error. If an error is made, or a previous assembler's error overlooked, the typewriter, shuffling down a straight line the length of two football fields, is soon out of sight. The offender need no longer care about it—: let the inspector worry.

Around 1969, at the climax of a prosperous decade, the demand for typewriters was straining our capacities—especially in Amsterdam, which fed the booming market of Europe. At the same time, Amsterdam felt intensely a new problem afflicting us all: A wave of young hires, more educated than their predecessors, were showing disdain for robot-like, programmed work. Absenteeism for "illness" was a constant disrupter. In droves, youngsters left their jobs soon after they were trained. Morale surveys were depressing.

As native-born youngsters grew hard to hire and harder to keep, the Amsterdam management welcomed the availability of immigrants from Turkey, the West Indies, southern Italy, Spain, and Morocco, who were attracted to northern Europe by a labor shortage and good wages. This trend, of course, presented a new set of problems in communication and cultural differences, blocking these newcomers from a sense of belonging. Without belonging there can be no sense of responsibility, and vice versa.

Our Amsterdam managers, acknowledging a crisis, gathered together in meeting after meeting, coming up with all sorts of explanations and corrective ideas. But each idea led to these questions: "How about the people who do the work? What do *they* think is wrong? What ideas do they have?"

The managers decided to take the most vital kind of "morale survey" of all. They began meeting with small groups of people, sometimes as few as two or three operators. They'd throw out a managerial idea or two, but would purposely emphasize a search for negatives by asking "What's wrong?" The sum total of what they consistently heard was that people resented feeling they were cogs in a long machine. They felt they were 60, 75, 100 people who scarcely knew each other, putting pieces of metal together with scarcely any sense of shared responsibility for the final product.

As these negative criticisms shifted to positive hopes, what came out with equal consistency was a desire by the people to have a longer work span with increased individual responsibility. This evolved into a picture of smaller work groups with stronger group and product identification—the psychology of a sports team.

The managers then took another step. They brought production engineers into the discussions—which led to a surprise: They found that the engineers and assemblers could communicate well. They could create ideas together, run into problems, and then figure out solutions together.

Within weeks these discussions led to a concept, created largely by the assembly people themselves, of a mini-line. This line, occupying a 13-yard-square space, was shaped like the sketch in Figure 6. The subassemblies entered the flow at the left side of the M-shaped line, making their way on roller conveyors through and around the M, until a finished typewriter was final-adjusted on the right side. Each of the 20 people could see—or could easily communicate with—all the others.

Once they received the subassemblies, the mini-line people were responsible for every phase of producing a typewriter except packing. They ordered their own parts from the ware-

Figure 6. Mini-line in Amsterdam plant.

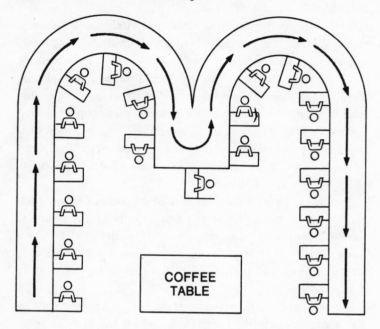

house, stored them at their work stations, and kept track to insure adequate supply. This was a new responsibility for assemblers—and they liked it.

They also took individual responsibility for functional mechanisms such as carriage return or backspacing. This responsibility included assembly, adjustment, and inspection of the mechanism, thus eliminating the end-of-line inspector—who is both the assembler's bane and crutch.

Moreover, the mini-line people decided that the best place for a new person to be trained was within the group itself. The "oldsters" in the group, having climbed the ladder of skills, could best teach the tricks of the trade; the entire group had a stake in how well a beginning assembler learned his basic work.

A pilot mini-line was installed in April 1970. It had its problems. Some operators, long accustomed to three-minute work segments, were less adept than others at learning to combine several operations into a ten-minute segment. Divisions of the work had to be adjusted and readjusted to keep the typewriters moving evenly. The most difficult problem, not entirely solved at this writing, was reorienting first-line managers. While most assemblers and upper-level managers embraced the possibilities, first-line managers suffered an upheaval in their concept of their job. They had been forced to busy themselves for hours with "time claiming"—keeping meticulous daily efficiency records of how many minutes each of dozens of assembly operations contributed to the total labor of each typewriter. (I had long wondered whether these records did not themselves contribute a significant cost to the finished product. We were soon to surmise that they did.)

Relieved of all this bookkeeping, the manager now had to manage people. Shorn of an end-of-line inspector, the manager was now personally responsible for the quality as well as quantity of what his people produced. Each of the people, in turn, could not evade responsibility for what *he* produced. If a person's work too often was defective, the manager now had the people-management task of finding out whether the person at fault had a training problem, a personal problem, an interpersonal problem, an equipment or supply problem, or whatever—and had to work out with that person what to do about it. And, it might be added, solution of the problem was now a concern of every member of the group.

For a time, output of the pilot mini-line fell below the manhour equivalent on the long line. But management was convinced of the advantages of the concept. A second mini-line was installed in September 1970, and a third and fourth in January 1971. Soon plant employees were requesting that more such lines be created so they could work on them. The Amsterdam management committed itself fully to mini-lines, initiating a full-year program to retrain all typewriter assemblers for the expanded work segments.

The productivity results of that high-risk commitment, even

though all the human adjustment problems have not been solved, have been spectacular. The switchover was completed in August 1971, and by the end of 1972 productivity had risen 35 percent—a net rise attributable purely to the mini-line. By the end of 1973, productivity was up 40 percent. Quality is more consistently high. Downtime for repairs has dropped tremendously: Assemblers make their own minor repairs, and a technician, himself a member of the group, has a stake in promptly attending to a co-worker's problem. An unanticipated benefit has been a substantial drop in product handling time—simply because the typewriter does not have to be pushed along as much as it did on the long line. Most important, in 1971 the employee attrition rate was 35 percent below what it had been in 1970; in 1972 it was more than 65 percent below the 1970 level. Management attributes this to a sharp and visible improvement in morale, although some of the attrition reduction owes itself to an economic slowdown in Europe at that time.

There are additional benefits that are not statistically measurable. During one sharp rise in production demand, word got out that the assembly procedure might be slightly reorganized to enable some of the work to be subcontracted out. Some of the people, fearing their groups might be broken up, were not very happy. They suggested higher output goals—and met them. One assembler, an IBMer since 1968, summed up our belief that total responsibility is an answer to boredom when she commented, "The monotony has passed. I sometimes feel as if I have my own small shop."

Within a year after the Amsterdam commitment, our Toronto plant began its own experimentation with mini-lines. This led to even more radical departures from the past.

Toronto had two parallel long lines, each with 60 people. The first half of each line was a department composed of 30 assemblers, including a technician (usually a top-producing operator who had been promoted to troubleshooter and repairman). The second half, another department, consisted of 30 adjusters and testers, including a technician.

Problems were similar to those in other plants: A jam-up of typewriters at any point on the line slowed all operations before and after it; and assemblers in the first half of the line virtually never saw finished machines, so felt little connection with the final product. In fact, an assembler felt little connection with the co-worker immediately behind and ahead of him. He was visually shielded from the next person by a parts bin on his workbench. The only person steadily in view was his counterpart on the adjacent parallel line, who was not a co-worker on the same typewriter. (Sometimes differences in their work rates led to animosities, rather than productive competition.) Finally, the long line of fragmented tasks, fraught with jam-up potential, was not easily conducive to stepping up production during peak demand periods.

The Toronto managers, in consultation with operators on the line, worked out a mini-line not of 20 people but of 10— and shaped like a U rather than an M. Figure 7 is a diagram of the line.

As in Amsterdam, the new small-team arrangement seemed to invite new forms of cooperation. More experienced people, now in easy contact with the less experienced, took on a tutoring role. If the technician was busy when a technical problem arose, another experienced person stepped in to keep things moving. The work area measured only 12′ × 40′, so a jam-up was visible to all—and became everyone's problem.

This "mini-mini-line" of ten people offered still another important advantage. If a rise in production demand appeared reasonably long-term, all that was required was the relatively easy setting up of another ten-person line.

As one of the Toronto managers commented, "We were looking for higher quality and making people more satisfied in their work. If we got that and just broke even on production, that would have been good enough. But we're making money at it."

Figure 7. U-shaped mini-line consisting of 10 people.

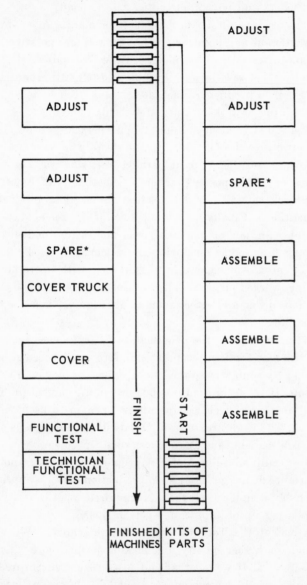

* Spare benches are for training.

If those achievements could be made by cutting a line from sixty to ten, had the end of the road been reached? The Toronto people asked themselves that question—and then set up a line of *six* people to build an entire typewriter. After a trial period, they found (1) that it could be done; (2) that the six-man line apparently could equal the productivity of the ten-man line, but with no practical promise of exceeding it; and (3) that the six people derived a strong satisfaction and sense of responsibility from their expanded jobs, but not perceptibly more than did those on the ten-man line.

The tentative conclusion of the Toronto people is that a six-person "micro-line," while feasible, offers no advantage for ordinary purposes. But it may hold important promise as a method for handling production peaks, or for transitional periods during production increases before a commitment is made to set up a permanent new ten-person mini-line.

I would like to conclude this discussion of mini-lines with a prediction. Heretofore in this book, much emphasis has been placed on individual rewards and individual motivation. I have also emphasized the importance of constant change—setting new goals, being sensitive to new opportunities that derive from solutions of old problems. I think it is quite possible that mini-lines will expand the possibilities for another form of motivation in the workplace. Mini-lines in production may very well correspond in motivational power to teams in sports. The player on a football eleven or baseball nine is no less motivated than the singles player in tennis. He wants his team to win just as much as the solo player wants to win. Apparently, it's when a team or group grows far beyond a dozen or so that individual drive becomes diluted.

In Lexington, we have already witnessed experimental mini-line groups giving themselves competitive names like "Tex's Rangers," named after that group's manager. In Amsterdam, one mini-line group decorated its area with plants. Group members spent spare time building planter boxes at home, even bringing in a planter-box tree that threatens to reach the ceiling. Other mini-lines began to do likewise. One competitive group, not satisfied to be imitators, installed an aquarium with live fish. This inspired another group to build a hutch housing live rabbits. At that point, a concerned management stepped in with some quiet words of discouragement. But I'm sure they were pleased by the signs of constructive competitive spirit, as any manager would be.

TOTAL RESPONSIBILITY
A VERTICAL STRUCTURE
OF MANAGEMENT

If the concept of total responsibility is to bring the best out of people, it must apply to the *structure of management* as well as to the design of individual jobs. Total responsibility in management means vertical management.

For clarification, let's turn to my friend the janitor again. The end product of his work is a clean plant. His complaint was that he performed a single *function* toward that end and that he had no control over the other functions. As a sweeper for the entire plant, his job was designed horizontally. What he wanted was vertical responsibility—control of all the cleaning functions in one part of the plant. Logically, he would then report to a manager in charge of the entire plant's cleanliness, who in turn might report to the plant's maintenance chief. If, on a given morning, most of the plant was clean but a small part of it was not clean, the cleaning manager would know exactly where the failure was, exactly the person whose work had to be improved.

Translating that idea to production, vertical management means putting a manager in charge of a product from beginning to end, and putting each submanager in charge of a single production group doing a specific phase of the work from beginning to end. In product support groups, it means putting a manager in charge of a service procedure from beginning to end.

I have explained our system of vertical management to many executives of other companies, and they usually nod and say, "Oh yes, we do that, too. We hold a department manager responsible for everything in his department. If something goes wrong, he's in trouble." That may be an effective way to pin blame when you can't really pin down whom to blame, but it is not necessarily vertical management. When I query these executives, it almost always turns out that their departments are organized horizontally—by function.

This confusion between horizontal and vertical management is common, but the difference is crucial. In a leading management magazine I recently read an article called "Tearing Down Departmental Walls." Perhaps the author thought he was pleading for vertical management. It was illustrated by a picture of a handsome, determined, managerial-looking fellow with rolled-up sleeves, ripping down plaster and smashing the lathe strips of a departmental wall. As I read through the article, I began to feel sorry for the fellow. His work was futile.

"Your problem, if you haven't caught on yet," the article said, "is that your firm's departments are separated by walls —invisible walls, maybe, but every bit as real as if they were made of concrete and steel. And until you tear them down your company will be beset with all the problems enumerated here."

What kinds of problems? The kinds that arise, said the article, from having autonomous departments of specialists (purchasing, engineering, production control, inventory control, warehousing, etc.)—all horizontal—and of having "these little men with their territories all staked out," each man protecting himself by "creating problems for all the other departments," sometimes at great cost.

And how are these problems to be eliminated? By a "total systems approach" in which "all these functions come under the watchful eye and the guidance of one man at the top"—at the top of a group of related functions. For example, according to the article, all purchasing, warehousing, production scheduling, and product inventory through to distribution would

> . . . come under the watchful eye and the guidance of . . . something like a "materials manager." Unlike the autocrat, however, the materials manager doesn't evaluate each department's separate performance but, instead, how well each department *harmonizes and coordinates* with all other departments. This one man brings all department leaders together, makes them realize they are all part of one function, all working toward one common goal, and offers each of them a say in how the job ought to be done—on an ongoing basis.

That is not a design for tearing down departmental walls. It just reconstructs the walls with thinner plaster, permitting sounds to pass from one horizontal department to another. Like an orchestra conductor, the materials manager tries to "harmonize and coordinate" the sounds into some kind of sweeter music. But the discords—the clashing functions of specialists, none of them responsible for an end product— remain. The only way to tear down departmental walls between functions is to tear down functional departments.

That's what we did with considerable success in producing typewriters, and subsequently in producing our other office products. When we were still organized horizontally at Lexington, we had three major assembly lines for the typebar typewriter. Each function—assembly, preadjusting, aligning, final adjusting, and so on—had a first-line manager whose responsibility spread across all three lines for that function. Each of these managers reported to a project manager—the one for his function. (There was a project manager for assembly, across all three assembly lines; one for the function of preadjusting, across all three lines; etc.—making a total of three project managers and 18 first-line managers.) Organizationally, this was exquisitely neat. But it was troublesome as could be. Talk about "men with their territories all staked out"! The manager for final adjustment would yell at some manager down the line, "You're sending me junk." The other manager would reply, "You worry about your job and I'll worry about mine." Rather than "harmonize and coordinate," both managers passed the buck to still another horizontal department: final inspection. That is the way most American manufacturing is organized—and, for a time, so were we.

Then we reorganized all responsibility *vertically* on these old-style long assembly lines. Starting from the bottom, each operator was made responsible insofar as possible for a specific task, as described in the previous chapter. His first-line manager was made responsible for a group of tasks in a *single* production line (a phase of assembly, adjusting, aligning, etc.). The assembly line now had six such first-line managers instead of the partial attention of 18. They reported to a project manager who had total responsibility for *one* assembly line—for the quantity and quality of every machine produced on that line, for every person who worked on that line. The three project managers (one for each line) reported to a product manager, responsible for the plant's total production of typebar typewriters. (There was another product manager for the Selectric, still another for the dictating machine, the Copier, etc.) Thus the organization of people—and the responsibility of people—was by end product, not by specialized function.

Instead of "harmonizing and coordinating," which inevitably means singing a chorus of excuses, we now had specific *accountability*. No one along the entire chain of responsibility could escape it. In fact, we were able to computerize accountability. If a Customer Engineer, upon opening a box, found a defect in a finished machine, he reported it to our plant and within minutes the serial number told us which assembly line was responsible. The type of defect told us which manager in charge of which phase of production was responsible and, in fact, which operator was responsible.

Tough? A system for laying blame? That is not the way people looked at it at all. For the opposite is also true. It is a system for recognizing good work as well—for rewarding people who consistently put out their best. It is a system in which no individual gets lost—his good work or poor work is a matter of record.

Vertical management is not limited to the assembly line, but reaches out with immense ramifications. A prime example is the machine floor, which is physically far removed from the assembly lines and in many large plants is a crisis center.

The Lexington machine floor is a spread of about four acres. Before we reorganized it, it was laid out in traditional fashion —separate department areas for primary punch presses, secondary punch presses, broaching, drilling, screw machines, burring, milling, grinding, straightening, and so on. Aisles between these departments were traffic jams of fork-lift trucks hauling partly completed jobs from one department to another. In the nerve center—or, more accurately, the nervous center— of the machine floor sat a group of production expediters. These expediters didn't run the floor, however. They were troubleshooters for the people who really ran it from a quarter mile away: the production control department. Production control exercised its "responsibility" for the machining of parts not by direct contact with the jobs but by analyzing computer printouts—8.2 miles of printouts per month.

Although it is traditional, sacrosanct, and virtually never questioned, this machine-floor layout is insane. Look at what happens. The computer instructs production control that it's time to machine 12,000 pieces of Part No. 9876. Production control prepares a routing sheet detailing the step-by-step, department-by-department process that must be followed to machine the 12,000 parts. The slip is dispatched to the raw stores, ordering metal to be sent to the primary-punch-press manager. That manager, already loaded with orders for a bewildering variety of parts, looks at the routing sheet and files it behind his other orders. As he completes each job, he calls production control to ask, "What do you want me to do next?" When he finally gets Part No. 9876 done, he sends for a truck to deliver the goods, say, to the burring department. From there it goes to secondary punch press, from there to grinding, from there to drilling, and so on, until finally the finished parts are delivered to the stockroom.

Every part number—out of thousands upon thousands—has a different routing. Every load of parts may travel miles, to and fro, before finally landing in the stockroom. One machine department gets hopelessly jammed with work to do, while another department runs out of work. Every time a load is moved, a punch card must be prepared to inform the computer of the movement—so the computer can answer production control when the assembly manager calls up to scream, "Where the hell are those parts? If I don't get them I'm going to have to shut down."

Suppose Part No. 9876 is in the punch press department and 9,000 of the 12,000 pieces have been stamped out when the die goes dull. The die is removed from the press and is sent to the toolroom. If the die can be sharpened right away, the punch press manager decides to wait for it, perhaps two hours —a machine and man standing idle. If the toolroom is backed

Production Control

up with work, the punch press manager will decide to suspend the job, setting up the machine with another die for another order. The last thing he would think of would be to send the 9,000 finished pieces as a completed order to the next operation when the routing slip calls for 12,000—the computer would go out of its mind.

Meanwhile, production control and the production expediters have "hot lists" of urgently needed parts to keep assembly lines going. The expediting of these parts intensifies the chaos in every department, in every aisle. *No department manager is responsible for any part.* The expediter tries to put out fires for production control; production control responds to the fire alarms of the computer. Who's responsible? The computer?

From 1962 to 1964 we revolutionized the organization of the machine floor—for total responsibility by every department manager. We set up 20 departments, each of about 20 people and a manager. No longer specialized by type of machine, every department was a self-sufficient machine shop— a small complex of punch presses, screw machines, milling machines, and so on. Each department was given total responsibility for, say, 250 part numbers—*all* the machining operations of those part numbers, from raw material to finished parts.

With this relatively small list of parts, it is possible for a manager and his machinists to learn intimately the procedures, the tolerances, the idiosyncracies of tools demanded by every part number—never possible when a department performs a single operation for thousands of part numbers. What a boon to quality control! Quality, quantity, production scheduling, and delivery—these became the total responsibility of one department manager.

Organizing such departments requires analysis and planning. When parts were assigned to a department, they were grouped by type. Insofar as possible, we also tried to group parts according to their end product. Ideally, one machine department devotes itself entirely to making 250 part numbers for the typebar typewriter (not for the Selectric, Copier, etc.). That department manager can then be totally responsive to the needs of a single assembly manager. He can develop close communication with that one man instead of enduring the chaos of conflicting and competing demands of several production schedules.

Under this system of total responsibility, a department manager is given a standing order for Part No. 9876 of, say, 800 a day. In one run, the manager may decide to produce a two-week supply, a three-week supply, whatever is best for his total production schedule. In this case, if he decides on a run of 12,000 and a tool goes dull after 9,000, he can suspend production on that part—and turn to another with no lost time. Finished parts are stored in *his own* stockroom in his own area—no more central inventory. He knows by his naked eye when his supply of any part is running low. He has total responsibility for shipping the proper quantity and quality of finished parts to the proper assembly line. He meets that responsibility—or his department will soon have a new manager.

When we first discussed this reorganization, some people foresaw terrible problems—as some people always do when an innovation is proposed. Most of the problems foreseen were exaggerated or never materialized. Furthermore, a good innovation often turns up advantages that no one anticipated. In this case, the traffic jam of truckers was reduced. No more endless trucking from punch presses to milling machines to grinding, etc., skidload upon skidload for thousands of parts. We needed only two shipments: one of raw materials to a department, and one of finished parts to an assembly line. We got rid of many trucks and retrained truckers for other jobs. The paperwork of move tickets, punch cards, send-aheads, and inventory record keeping was slashed. There was nothing to route—because material stayed in a department until finished parts were shipped out.

Expediters? The department manager, totally responsible

for his parts from beginning to end, became his own expediter. Production control's function was greatly reduced. Quality control was now built into production itself. Inventories of machined parts were reduced 35 percent, and most important of all, assembly lines seldom went hungry for parts.

That is what vertical management—and total responsibility —can accomplish. The more it is extended, the more it accomplishes. We have extended it beyond the assembly line, beyond the machine-floor departments, and into a structure of vertical organization for each *total end product*.

To examine how vertical organization by product works, let's look at one such organization, that of the typebar typewriter in our Berlin plant. It is headed by a product manager. Reporting to him are two project managers, one for assembly and one for production support.

The project manager for assembly is in charge of six assembly mini-lines, each consisting of 20 to 25 assemblers, each headed by a first-line manager. The project manager for production support is responsible for insuring that the assembly department is supplied with parts and subassemblies. He is also responsible for their quality. He has authority to subcontract for parts or assemblies when his in-plant facilities are overloaded. He reports directly—and only—to the product manager. The job of his department is to do what is necessary to keep the typewriter assembly department operating without interruption.

Under this project manager for support are groups for procurement, engineering, quality engineering, inventory management, and dispatch (which includes storage of finished inventory). Again, all these project groups are concerned solely with typebar typewriters—not plantwide functions. Even storage of parts has been decentralized according to end product. Parts are stored near the assembly line or, when feasible, within it. Dispatchers pull the parts into the assembly lines without any paperwork.

As the Berlin product manager for typebar typewriters

recently summed up this method of organization to me, "It used to be that when I had a problem I'd have to bring together five or six people. The quality man would say it's a manufacturing problem. The manufacturing man would say it's an engineering problem, that the specs should be changed. Everybody defined his function, but nobody solved the problem. Now I talk to one man. It certainly saves a lot of discussion."

In Lexington we were, until recently, producing five product groups under a single roof—the typebar typewriter, the Selectric, dictating products, electronic products, and chemical products. This vertical system meant that, for example, we. had five separate purchasing departments, each linked to its own production control and quality control.

Actually, there was a sixth as well: a man in plantwide Administrative and Financial Services who looked after overall purchasing. Aha! A functional or horizontal "coordinator"! But not so. That man had nothing to do with negotiating with vendors, the size of orders, or anything of that sort. Actually, he was charged with two things—making sure that product purchasing groups conformed to company policy regarding handling of vendors, and making sure that separate purchasing groups did not unwittingly overload our dependence on any vendor.

Soon after we verticalized purchasing, I visited some of our major vendors to get their reaction to dealing with several buyers from our plant, each with an intimate knowledge of a single product. Did they prefer the old way of dealing with one commodity buyer? Without exception, they said, "Let us deal with someone who knows the end product. Sometimes we're given a tolerance on a part that kills us, or we have some idea for improving a part. If the man knows the product, he can give us an answer. We know the commodity and the manufacturing process."

It also developed that buyers for a single product suggested direct savings that a plantwide buyer might often miss. The plantwide buyer tends to buy what production control orders. The single-product buyer, instructed by production control to buy 10,000 of some item, is more likely to take notice upon learning that he can get a price break at, say, 15,000. Being in direct daily contact with a single-product manager, he is better able to evaluate the feasibility of buying the larger quantity. Also, as a member of a product team he is more motivated and better able to suggest engineering changes to help meet cost goals.

Horizontal-function groups have a way of breeding on themselves. Because they are fundamentally inefficient and cause unnecessary problems, they expand, adding new specialists and coordinators to solve the problems their inefficiency causes. In contrast, we have found that vertically organized groups tend to seek out inefficiencies and tighten lines against them.

An example is the invention by one of our Berlin product managers of what we call a "super-buyer." Generally a plant has a buyer, a manufacturing engineer, and a quality engineer all dealing with a single vendor. They usually specialize in a type of part or type of commodity rather than an end product. In addition, a product engineer may have secondary contact with the vendor. Upon changing to a vertical, product-oriented organization, the Berlin people "verticalized" purchasing, creating a purchasing group to buy for a single product.

But what did not meet the eye at first was that the group was still divided by functions. At about that time, we had started a campaign for all plants to reduce the ratio of "indirect" (or support) people to "direct" (or hands-on) manufacturing people. This raised the question: Why did a single product require three functional specialists to deal with vendors? How many conflicts could be avoided among these spe-

cialists, how many meetings canceled, how many files combined, and how much paperwork eliminated if a single buyer
who knew our end product was trained in the special functions
required so that he was expert in all the requirements of buying parts for it?

Since all the men performing these purchasing functions
had backgrounds in engineering, they were capable of learning
thoroughly the parts requirements for our product. The product manager proposed to his purchasing people the idea of a
super-buyer with full responsibility for negotiating with a
vendor on matters of price, specifications, quality, delivery,
and so on. One man volunteered to be trained as the first experimental super-buyer. For several weeks he actually worked
on the production line to get ''fingertip'' familiarity with the
parts of his product—how they function, how they are put
together, what may make them fail. This added up to intimate
awareness of what makes a purchased part or assembly acceptable for use. It also equipped him to deal with the vendor on
such fine points as design, tolerances, and manufacturing
processes.

Today, three super-buyers are handling a purchasing volume which, in the estimation of the product manager, would
require a minimum of four men under the old specialized
system.

Following up the apparent success of the super-buyer experiment, the Berlin people are now experimenting with combining two other jobs—the purchasing administrator and the
production control person. A purchasing administrator prepares purchase orders for vendors and keeps a purchase history of vendors and part numbers. A production control person's job appears to be the opposite, but is actually closely
related. He keeps tabs on the in-plant demand for parts, develops availability schedules, and notifies the purchasing administrator of replenishment needs. When functionally separated, these two people have to work closely, interdependently,
requiring excellent personal communication. Actually, one of

the chief skills both people require is the ability to get along with each other.

At the Berlin plant, with minimal training one man was able to learn both jobs. This eliminated the need to communicate, combined files, eliminated paperwork, and reduced the possibility of error. At this writing, the combined job is working very satisfactorily.

10

TOTAL RESPONSIBILITY
AT WHAT MANAGERIAL
LEVEL?

We just looked at examples of producing economy and efficiency by combining responsibilities into one job. But that's not always the way to economy and efficiency. Sometimes vertical management requires the *creation* of a job, either by adding or splitting, as a way to focus responsibility properly. We found this particularly true with regard to the management of a major piece of capital equipment and the three people who operated it.

The power frame of the typewriter is machined on a huge transfer machine. The machine is more than 100 feet long and automatically performs about 250 operations—drilling holes, tapping holes, milling, boring, spot facing, and so on. A raw casting as taken from a mold is put into the mammoth machine, which transfers the piece from one operation to another in a great circle, and out comes the completed power frame. We have three of these transfer machines in Lexington and one in Amsterdam. The first one, which we bought in 1957, cost about $750,000. At this writing we are planning to purchase a fifth machine to be installed in our Canadian plant—at a cost approaching $3 million. Downtime of so expensive and complex a machine, while unavoidable, must be kept to a minimum through constant attention to maintenance and tooling.

To be perfectly consistent with our plan of vertical management, that huge machine should be in a machining department, with its maintenance, quality control, production scheduling, etc., handled by the department manager and his technician-assistant. But each machining manager already has about 20 people to worry about, people who operate milling machines, drilling machines, and so on. The transfer machine requires undiluted attention if it's to pay for itself. Someone has to take total responsibility for it.

What we did was to constitute the transfer machine and its three people as a department, adding the cost of a manager with that specific responsibility. For example, that manager and his three men watch the condition of drills and cutters and schedule their sharpening to best fit in with production demand. They also control the inventory of raw castings and finished power frames. Along comes a high-demand period when typewriters are back-ordered. The product manager informs the transfer machine manager, "You've been running at 2,000 a day. We must have 2,500 a day. Work out with your three men how you are going to take care of it." No big conclaves with production specialists. His responsibility is clear.

Three months after departmentalizing the transfer machine

with its own manager, we ran a cost analysis of the new system versus the old. The study found that setup time and need for engineering aid were reduced and productivity was increased. The increase enabled us to keep up with a rising demand for power frames while postponing for a year the purchase of the additional transfer machine.

Was it worth adding the salary of a manager to supervise only a three-person department? The net saving for a year—after deducting the manager's salary from what we saved plus the added quantity produced per day—came to $125,000.

That example illustrates a basic principle that flows from total responsibility and vertical management: *Responsibility should be assigned to the lowest-ranking manager possible.*

Put another way, responsibility should be placed where the work is done. Otherwise, you have the work being done on one level, the responsibility resting on another.

There are many ways in which a department can be organized to follow that principle. In analyzing the principle, our Toronto people came up with the conclusion that a first-line manager—the lowest-ranking manager in the product organization, in charge of a single mini-line—should be able to run it virtually as his own small, independent business. He should have total responsibility for production, quality, cost, engineering, and parts control.

Traditionally, the first-line manager was responsible only for an assembly group of 10 to 15 people who directly built the product. Under the new "small business" system, he is given two staff people, each to oversee a function that had previously been a separate plantwide or productwide function. These two new staff jobs are called production control and engineering control. The production control person is responsible for auditing, expediting, stock clerking, production planning, and the administration of engineering change. The engineering control person is responsible for production engineering, assembly engineering, quality engineering, and methods engineering. Since they report solely to the first-line manager and he works closely with them, the manager himself learns the critical details of these functions and how they mesh, an education he never had an opportunity to acquire when production control and engineering control were placed somewhere else, several levels above his authority. Thus the manager is truly in command of his business, as any small businessman must be.

When this system was first tried on an assembly line, the Toronto people assumed that the manager would need two men for production control and two for engineering control, since those responsibilities had always been so complex and time-consuming at higher echelons. But they soon found that one man could handle each job—and more. The first-line manager's job was so greatly simplified that he was able to take on the added responsibility of what amounted to an additional assembly line: a group of 13 people who recondition trade-ins of typebar and Selectric typewriters. His two assistants have been able to absorb the production control and engineering control of that group, too.

This expansion of responsibility has produced still another fall-out benefit. Since the assembly line and the reconditioning group both work under the same manager, that manager (aided by his two assistants) is better able to cope smoothly with peaks and dips in the demand for typewriter production. During peaks he transfers people from reconditioning to production; during dips he does the reverse.

The efficiencies are many, all deriving from placing responsibility on the level where the work is done. Warehouse paperwork has been slashed. Under the old system, parts, shipped to Toronto from Lexington, would go to a central stockroom; weekly releases of parts to each assembly line required mountainous record keeping. Now these parts are transferred directly from the unloading dock to the assembly area, where they are receipted by the production control person and stored near the assembly line.

Perhaps as valuable a benefit as any is the fact that the

"small businessman" and his two lieutenants are learning more, earlier in their careers, than people of comparable rank have an opportunity to do under the traditional system. Thus they are accelerating their future value to the company and their own qualifications for advancement.

The small-business principle is being applied in a somewhat different but very promising way by the Amsterdam plant. They have created a "small business" for the production of a product within the product. It might be called total responsibility within total responsibility.

The Selectric typewriter, which Amsterdam makes for a large portion of the world, has a mechanism called the carrier-and-rocker. This mechanism, which transports the typehead (the plastic ball on which the typefaces are molded), is intricate, precise, and costly. It represents about 10 percent of the cost of the entire machine. Out of the approximately 500 assemblers in Amsterdam who build the entire Selectric, about 35 work on the carrier-and-rocker. Somehow the carrier-and-rocker has always been a kind of "stepchild," needing special attention for its special problems but never quite getting it from the engineers, quality controllers, production controllers, and buyers, who generally have many other things to worry about.

The Amsterdam management separated the carrier-and-rocker from the production of the typewriter itself, setting it up as an independent unit with its own first-line manager. He has total responsibility for delivering carriers-and-rockers to three product groups—the Selectric and its two modifications which are separate products, the Composer and electronically controlled typewriters. He has his own support group for engineering, production control, quality control, purchasing, record keeping, and so on. Being, in a sense, an in-house subcontractor himself, he has authority to subcontract parts of his job out of house. In short, he has the flexibility of a product manager.

The advantages, in the early stage of this experiment, appear to be (1) a reduced cost of indirect (or support) services in relation to direct work; (2) a noticeable rise in morale of all the people in the group, including operators, resulting from their small-business feeling and the special reliance placed on them; (3) the carrier-and-rocker, no longer a stepchild, gets the full attention and expertise of its engineers, buyers, etc.; and (4) the product manager for the Selectric may now concentrate on improving other areas of his organization.

As one of the Amsterdam managers speculated to me recently, "If 10 percent of the cost can be separated this way— a troublesome 10 percent—and problems get solved, how about *other* 10 percents?"

In fact, other troublesome parts have already "gone into business for themselves" under their own manager. Take the IBM Composer, a complex product produced in relatively small quantities. Assembly of the Composer never got the attention it deserved simply because the machine was a part of the Selectric assembly lines. Also, the supporting people, such as engineers and production control people, were part of the Selectric support groups.

The Composer has now been separated from these groups and brought under the control of one overall Composer manager who has complete responsibility for every aspect of production. The product now gets the full attention of its supporting people, which gives them an opportunity to simplify procedures and working methods to fit the specific needs of the product. This has saved indirect effort and has built a team of people whose self-supporting attitude would be difficult to beat.

Still another area where the Amsterdam people have set up a small-business unit is the cover painting department. This department paints and subassembles the covers for the Amsterdam products. For years, technical and planning problems made this department a trouble spot in the plant. Several attempts were made to clear up the situation, but there was no real improvement until the department was set up as a separate group, with both support and production combined under one manager.

The responsibility for inventory, painting, and the subassembly of covers is now concentrated in one small-business unit. The manager has full authority to organize his "business" his own way, as long as he keeps the assembly lines supplied with the right covers at the right time.

The team spirit and involvement of these people are so great that today they not only have overcome the troubles associated with cover painting and subassembling but are working on improvements in other areas.

A few pages back I stated the principle, disquieting as it may be to some, that responsibility should be assigned to the lowest ranking manager possible. Responsibility should be placed where the work is done. If that is to be followed to its logical conclusion, some absolutist might raise the ultimate question, "Why not place responsibility where the work *really* is done? Why not do away with the manager?"

It is true that some of a manager's duties may be delegated downward to operators, and perhaps some of them upward, to the point where that particular manager's job becomes superfluous. He could then be eliminated and his personnel responsibilities combined with those of another manager.

That actually has been done experimentally in one of our small plants in Boigny, France, about 60 miles south of Paris. The Boigny plant produces a variety of manufactured and printed products for several IBM divisions. Because the items are relatively simple, the case may be of special interest to companies engaged in such production.

The management changeover in Boigny chiefly involved the production of typewriter ribbons—the inking of sizable rolls of material, slicing the rolls to ribbon width, spooling them, and packing them. Previously the plant had an Office Products Division manager, responsible not only for the ribbons but also for a very different kind of product, the typehead (the Selectric typeface ball), which is molded on complex machinery. He had a production control unit with responsibility straddling both products—purchasing, materials storage and distribution, administration of orders, machine maintenance, and so on. Production itself was performed by several units of about a dozen people each; each group had a first-line manager. We "verticalized" those products, putting a product manager in charge of each product and giving each product manager his own production control unit.

A changeover, even such a relatively simple one, tends to force examination of other questions when a management is inquiring and ambitious—which the people in Boigny are. One of the concerns that came out in response to this changeover was that the work in the ribbon department was particularly routine and repetitive. What might be done to make it less boring? Rejecting artificial gimmicks of "job enrichment," the Boigny managers asked themselves how, in real ways, they could increase the responsibility of the ribbon-makers.

One of the first things they analyzed was maintenance, which at that time was all performed by a separate maintenance department. They found that maintenance activities could be divided into three categories. First, there was a level of daily maintenance which any of the operators in ribbon-making was capable of learning. Second, there was a level of servicing and repair which the more experienced of the operators could be trained to do. Third was the relatively rare major service that definitely required a specialist from outside the department.

Maintenance duties were reorganized. The first two levels were brought into the production groups in the ribbon-making department. The third level remained with the maintenance department.

That step led to other questions. Couldn't the operators be given direct charge of their own raw materials and product inventory, even their own production record keeping? Of course.

That led to still another question: Since the production groups for typewriter ribbons were relatively small—about a dozen each—couldn't more groups report directly to the department manager? Did they really need a first-line manager to "manage" routines they could take charge of themselves? Or could they be organized as in Figure 8?

As shown in the figure, the groups report directly to the department manager. This is now being tried in several departments. The group can physically arrange its workplace any way it likes. It has responsibility for notifying the manager when new raw materials have to be ordered, and for coordinating people's tasks to meet a production schedule. Each person is expected to learn every job in the group, so that anyone can serve as a backup for anyone else.

The department manager, of course, maintains constant contact with the groups, with their problems and decisions, and has personnel responsibility for each individual in each group. But the spirit of the arrangement is such that he will not in-

Figure 8. Departmental organization in which production groups report directly to department manager (Boigny plant).

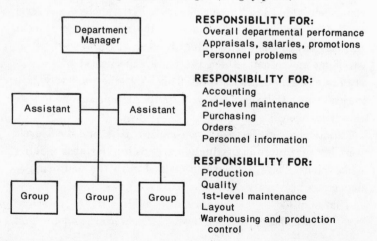

RESPONSIBILITY FOR:
Overall departmental performance
Appraisals, salaries, promotions
Personnel problems

RESPONSIBILITY FOR:
Accounting
2nd-level maintenance
Purchasing
Orders
Personnel information

RESPONSIBILITY FOR:
Production
Quality
1st-level maintenance
Layout
Warehousing and production
control

trude on day-to-day matters if the groups are meeting their production responsibilities and conforming to company personnel policies.

The objective of these changes was not an unusual rise in production output. During the groups' first year, 1972, their goal was to equal the previous year's output, which they did. The productivity benefits are sought from two directions: (1) savings in indirect services taken over by the groups, as well as in first-line managers' salaries; (2) the productivity gain that derives from reduced absenteeism and turnover because people are more satisfied.

Are the people more satisfied? Before it got under way, some were leery of the plan. In one group of 12, four—all of them women—expressed disinterest in taking part. This puzzled the Boigny management. One of the managers recalled reading a report of a similar experiment by an electronics concern at Eindhoven, Holland, in which it was found that there, too, men were more willing than women to try this particular change. The four Boigny women were given other jobs. A year after the new system had been established, no member had asked to be transferred out.

The possible merits of this group-responsibility system are indeed worth exploring. However, they do seem to require suspension of one of the principles advanced earlier in this book. Because responsibility is shared, production records are *group* production records. Therefore, there is no numerical way of identifying top producers. Pay rates in the Boigny ribbon-making groups span three pay levels. Promotion through these levels must be determined by the department manager's personal appraisal. This throws a special responsibility on the manager. Since group members are intimately involved with one another's work, they have an especially keen sense of who the best producers are. It is important to the morale of his people that the manager's decision be an informed and sensitive one.

Group responsibility and group achievement may in time

prove as great a motivator as personal responsibility—or a greater one. We see it in athletic teams. We see it in our mini-lines and "small business" units. But group responsibility— a system in which group production records are kept—may present a very difficult challenge to the judgment of managers. I can think of no surer way to destroy group motivation than allowing favoritism to creep back into a promotion system.

For years managers and management theorists have debated over an idea called "span of control." The consensus seems to be that a second-line manager (whose responsibility is hard to define) shouldn't have more than four to six people reporting to him, lest he lose control.

We took a good hard look at that at Lexington, and concluded that it was one of the worst ideas ever put over—and probably the most expensive. After all, in the case of the first-line manager, the toughest job of all, we normally don't want fewer than ten people in his charge (allowing for special exceptions, such as that of the transfer machine manager). People, whether managers or not, don't like to work under close supervision, and if they're properly trained and have clear-cut responsibility, they don't have to. Having someone constantly looking over your shoulder kills initiative and stifles productivity. This applies especially to managers with personal initiative.

Back at Lexington, our move to mini-lines, coupled with the concept of vertical management, has led us to take a hard look at our whole second level of management—the project-manager level. We announced to all our management people at Lexington an intention to have first-line managers, those in charge of each of the mini-lines, report directly to a third-level manager. That intention could not be accomplished overnight, because many second-line managers were involved. The whole tenor of our program depends on not hurting a single individual, so the program has had to move along at the rate at which we could find suitable new assignments for those people.

In the cases where we have effected this change, wonderful things have happened. Taking out one level of communication has enabled first-line managers to get more direct and therefore more accurate information, faster responses, and faster decisions (if the problem requires one). Also, their own voices have become more important.

In my early days as plant manager at Lexington, when we were still organized along traditional, horizontal lines, I often thought I would go out of my mind fighting fires. The assembly-line people would come to me hurting for parts. I would get them together with production control, who would blame it on purchasing, who in turn would blame it on quality control—the old merry-go-round.

After the reorganization, each product manager had his own "plant"—five small plants for five products, under the same roof, each self-sufficient. I had four service groups, not directly engaged in production, reporting to me: financial, personnel, manufacturing services, and production engineering. I also had a tight personal staff. Ten self-sufficient areas—and my job was never easier. Everybody knew what they were supposed to do. I'd have to take a trip and someone would ask, "Who's looking after the plant?" I'd reply, "My secretary. Call her, and whatever your problem is, she'll put you in touch with the right person."

During the period of our greatest growth, the mid-1960s, besides being plant manager I was also vice president of manufacturing for the domestic Office Products Division and, as such, had certain responsibilities regarding a new plant in Austin, Texas. In addition, I was director of manufacturing for IBM World Trade Office Products; this meant looking after seven other plants outside the United States. Carrying those three jobs, I was away from Lexington 60 percent of the time. Production grew, productivity grew, costs declined, and morale was high. Why? Because capable people—organized along lines of vertical management, with total responsibility —knew their jobs, were freed to do them, and did them well.

11

GOALS

One of the most confusing of all the confusions in business planning is a common tendency to confuse *methods* and *goals*. I remember a meeting we once had in Canada of some people from our worldwide plants in which we were pushing certain improved methods of purchasing. While we were planning this purchasing changeover, the air was suddenly filled with phrases like, "In order to accomplish this objective—" and "We've got to start selling our people on this goal—." Finally, one clear-minded young man said, "What we're talking about is not an objective at all. A method of purchasing is a method. An objective is to take two dollars out of the cost of the typewriter, and improved purchasing is one of the methods we use. Let's not confuse the two."

Almost every manager's bookshelf has a book on management by objectives. That's because every good manager knows that progress is accomplished only by realistic setting of goals, dividing these goals into departmental goals, and steaming everyone up to accomplish them. But the trouble with most of these books is that instead of starting at the starting line, they start somewhere near the finish line. You can't start just by setting an objective. Like runners in a cross-country race, people have to be prepared by long, carefully planned motivation and training.

That's what all the preceding chapters of this book have been about: methods to equip people for pursuit of goals. Merit pay and merit promotion are methods of motivation. We took many months putting in our system of merit pay—explaining how it worked, making sure everyone from top to bottom understood it, making sure that earned pay raises were given promptly, thus solidifying people's confidence that the system was honest and that it worked. Then we spent more months on merit promotion, on work simplification for efficiency, on workmanship analysis for quality. Then we worked on total responsibility and vertical management.

These were all vigorous campaigns—to equip ourselves with methods. Had they been confused with goals, they would have been illusions, evaporating into the thin air of little accomplishment. If work simplification had been considered a goal instead of a method, how would we measure achievement of the goal? By achieving 100 percent enrollment in work-simplification classes? That's not a real achievement. We could obtain 100 percent enrollment just by administrative edict, then go around congratulating ourselves for having achieved a goal. But what would that get us on the bottom line—in terms of increased efficiency and lowered cost? On the other hand, work simplification as a method equips us to set a specific *goal* of reduced cost. When we achieve that goal, we know the method has served us well.

Our first serious effort at goal setting came while most of these necessary preliminary programs were in effect or in process: Work-simplification classes were well under way and people were becoming their own efficiency experts. Also, we had just made our first major move toward vertical management, combining manufacturing engineering and production engineering into a single, more efficient group called production engineering. Savings were apparent almost immediately.

This first serious goal involved a new product we had just introduced, which had a projected year-end manufacturing cost of $175. After more thought, however, I had a hunch we could do better than that, particularly if we could drastically reduce the manufacturing expense rate in this product group. The manufacturing expense rate is the burdensome "indirect" cost riding on each product. This rate includes the cost of managers, stock handlers, paper pushers, purchased services, supplies, etc.—in short, all the overhead, which costs more per machine than the salaries of the people who physically put it together and the materials they use.

We concluded that if we could reduce the manufacturing expense rate to $6 for every manhour of direct work, and at the same time make the direct work more efficient, it would be feasible to set a goal of producing the machine for $160. Six dollars, $160; in a sense, those were two interrelated goals rolled into one. One fellow got the bright idea of calling the campaign "6/160."

The 6/160 slogan captured everyone's imagination and enthusiasm. (In fact, to this day, whenever we have a meeting on how costs can be reduced to achieve a new goal, it's still called a 6/160 meeting.) There's nothing like a succinctly stated, vivid, dramatic goal to stimulate people's desire to contribute.

We were a relatively new plant, eager to make a mark for ourselves in the company, hungry to grow. Every department went to work on its procedures to find where fat could be cut down to muscle and bone. Product engineers reviewed the design of every part and subassembly for possible simplifications. Manufacturing engineers went to work on more efficient procedures and equipment. Layout engineers reexamined assembly-line designs. The purchasing department, in cooperation with vendors, searched for new economies. Vendors came to meetings and were asked for ideas on cutting the costs of parts they produced. They suggested many changes in tolerances, tooling, and equipment. Assemblers, eager to use their new work-simplification skills to advance their own pay and promotion ambitions, were also fired up by the plantwide goal. All these efforts fused so beautifully that by the end of the year we had overshot the goal. We actually wound up with a $155 machine.

A cardinal rule of goal setting is that when a goal is accomplished another must be set. Having no goal to shoot at invites relaxation, mediocrity, and deterioration. Another rule is that only one goal should be pursued at a time. To the utmost degree possible, every plan, every meeting, every publicity effort, every competition and award, every ounce of management effort should somehow link with that goal and contribute to its accomplishment. The goal should be substantial enough to merit concentration for an extended period of time. We have found that one year is, for most major goals, a good period of time.

The 6/160 goal had called for a reexamination of every aspect of machine design and manufacture. The next year, having completed the full round of work-simplification classes, *alternating goals* we concentrated on improving work efficiency. The next year we worked on further expense reduction, linked to more advanced vertical-management reorganizations. Then we switched back to work efficiency. And so forth.

Sticking to one goal at a time, we always looked for the area where attention seemed most needed, and where concentrated attention might produce the greatest gain. Upon choosing our next goal, we would study and plan how to direct the whole factory force, from top to bottom, toward achieving it.

The next few years saw a series of yearly cost targets set and met. Our best achievement was December 1966, when the manufacturing cost of the typebar typewriter was down 45 percent from our starting cost in Kingston, New York, in 1956. This could not have been done without the ability to mobilize everyone working on the product to work toward their goals.

Manufacturing efficiency has remained virtually level since that achievement, though dollar costs, including labor, have since risen due to inflation. More troubling to us has been the rise in indirect costs, which have risen three times as rapidly as labor costs. (The attack we made on these indirect costs will be described in the next two chapters, on simplified business procedures.)

During the time when our cost goals were being accomplished, we heard that there was a widespread assumption— among our own people as well as some at higher headquarters —that the reduced costs, while fine, must be causing quality to suffer. We looked into this and found that quality was not declining at all. But the inquiry we had made convinced us that there was room for quality improvement. We had just completed our workmanship-analysis program, so we were tooled up for an all-out campaign to improve quality. Actually, this was a cost-cutting campaign as well as a quality-improving one. Since the factory was charged for service required under our 90-day warranty, we could reduce our costs by reducing warranty charges. We designed a one-year campaign with a specific goal: to cut warranty expense in half. We called it Project NEW—"No Expense for Warranty." (Catchy, but not as accurate as a good slogan should be.) We did cut the expense in half, thus reducing the cost of the typewriter, and since then we have further shaved warranty cost.

The setting of a goal, as observed earlier, is not the starting line. People must first be equipped with appropriate training and an efficient management structure for achieving it. But the setting of a goal is certainly not the finish line either. It is just the beginning of constant, concentrated work and attention.

Goal setting generally begins at the top of an organization and works its way down. The goal must be translated into subgoals for every department, every activity. Each department must know—and accept—what it must accomplish if the entire plant is to accomplish *its* overall goal. Thus an important pressure helps power the plantwide campaign. Nobody wants to get caught failing at his subgoal while others are accomplishing theirs. More positively, managers are rated for possible promotion and pay increases on their record of goal achievement, just as operators are rated on personal productivity.

There are many ways to stimulate managers into stretching their efforts for the accomplishment of goals. (And, needless to say, any goal should require people to stretch, or there's scarcely any point in setting one.) The simplest way, of course, is to rate a manager's achievement of a goal in straight percentages—95 percent, 105 percent, and so on. One of our overseas plants devised a more complicated system of awarding points, which has much to be said for it because it recognizes several dimensions of achievement. For meeting his goal of increased production and reduced cost (while maintaining standards of quality), a manager would earn 100 points. Top management believed, however, that a good campaign should also bring out new potentials of individuals—particularly their potential for ingenuity and innovation. A manager would be awarded additional points, to a maximum of 30, if members of his group came up with useful innovations. These would be evaluated by a plantwide committee. A manager could also earn points by good handling of upgradings and promotions in his area.

A campaign to accomplish a goal must include a system for getting feedback information. Every manager should know, at any point in time, how his actual production output, cost, etc., are measuring up against his monthly and annual goals. Otherwise he is exposed to rude surprises.

As plant manager, I used to schedule monthly meetings of all managers—400 people—and displayed charts showing how every product group was doing on efficiency, cost, quality, manufacturing expense, absenteeism, and so forth. Each product group would either pat themselves on the back or be embarrassed. But few would be surprised, because product groups were expected to hold mid-month meetings to check on their progress while there was still time to do something about it. These meetings also helped maintain a sense of urgency. Any lessening of urgency, especially when it emanates from the top of the organization, quickly leads to stagnation at all levels and deterioration of morale. Conversely, when a group stretches its efforts to achieve a goal and regularly knows its progress, high morale is virtually guaranteed.

In our plant, responsibility for accomplishing goals and subgoals penetrated down through the whole management structure, including the first-line-manager level. We also knew that first-line managers were calling monthly meetings with their people to discuss ways and means of achieving department goals.

Once we had to create a special goal: increased production of our electronically controlled typewriters in order to meet a demand surge. The reasons for the goal were explained to everyone; methods for achieving it were discussed by all. When the goal was reached, we threw a steak dinner for the couple of hundred people in that product group. Awards were distributed and everyone felt lifted by the recognition.

It's no small point that the product manager knew exactly who to invite to that party. Everybody involved in the goal was *totally* involved in it—through a vertically managed product organization. That product manager would have been in a terrible fix trying to shoot for a tough goal using separate, plantwide departments for engineering, production control, quality control, whatever. Goal setting and horizontal functions are incompatible. Perhaps that's why manufacturing plants seldom celebrate anything. In contrast, sales departments constantly set goals, accomplish them—and have more parties than any group in industry!

Goals have been discussed here not only as being *given,* but also as being *accepted.* A goal handed down as a command can bring resentment. In contrast, when a goal is proposed and managers are asked to evaluate it and to discuss ways and means of achieving it, the involvement makes the goal their own.

Extending this involvement below the managerial level often brings gratifying surprises. We had one such experience in our small plant—only about 50 people—in Bogotá, similar to the one in Amsterdam that I already described. The plant had a special order for some export typewriters which, if filled promptly, might open the way to a permanent increase in its export business. The Colombian government, in fact, had expressed a special interest in this order as a potential spur to the country's economy. Calling his people together, the plant manager explained the opportunity and further explained that since the surge might be temporary he planned to subcontract out most of the extra work. Next day, some of the people asked the manager if they could have another meeting. They had been thinking and talking about it since the previous day and felt confident they could handle the order themselves. They worked out a plan—and accomplished it. Managers keep underestimating the tremendous interest that people have in the success of their company.

A campaign does not mean artificial hoopla with propaganda and posters. Actually, we have always avoided posters, sticking to the strict principle that communication with the people should be through the first-line manager—personally and through small meetings. This not only spreads the feeling of responsibility but also tightens the organization, increasing the sense of teamwork.

Once a goal is set, top managers should be kept apprised

of the progress of managers at lower levels—but should respect their authority and responsibility. They must be left free to get their work done in their own way. One person with clear authority can accomplish more than ten people following each other around in a confused circle. Also, they must be protected from outside intrusions. I used to spend about a third of my time defending the plant from interference by higher headquarters. If that helped leave managers free to concentrate on their goals, it was time well spent.

Finally, a little constructive subterfuge we have always had fun with (and I suppose it goes on in most companies) : When the time of the year came around to set goals—or establish operating plans, as we more formally call them—we actually developed not one goal but two. One was a goal to submit to headquarters, and the other, a tougher one, was for ourselves. Amusingly, we began calling these ''in-house'' and ''out-house'' goals. The out-house goal—for headquarters—was always an improvement over the previous year's operation and looked reasonably hard to achieve. Headquarters would be pleased, sometimes a little skeptical as to whether we could reach it. Then we'd go to work having monthly meetings and mid-month meetings to achieve our tougher (and secret) in-house goal. So, year after year we'd do better than our operating plan as accepted by headquarters. This enabled us to establish and maintain complete credibility in headquarters for 15 years, which in itself made our work simpler because we spent less time justifying our proposals. All the way down through our organization, people enjoyed and took pride in the plant's reputation.

12

SIMPLIFIED BUSINESS PROCEDURES
DEACTIVATING THOSE COST GENERATORS

Art Buchwald, the political satirist, recently came up with a hilarious plan for reducing the cost of government. Most hilarity is drawn from truth—and Buchwald's "truth" applies to big business as well as to big government.

Bureaucracy will never be reduced, Buchwald points out, unless bureaucrats have an incentive to reduce it. Therefore he suggests that any government employee who figures out how to eliminate his own job should be retired at full pay for the rest of his life! Where's the profit to the taxpayer? Here comes the part of the scheme that's not so funny. For most employees—whether in government or business—a salary is only half the cost of a job, maybe less. The other half or more goes to space, light and heat, telephones and travel, file cabinets, typewriters, and computers, not to mention fringe benefits and the biggest cost of all—the paperwork that one unnecessary bureaucrat spends his time generating for other unnecessary bureaucrats.

On a grander scale Buchwald proposes that if an administrator figures out a way to abolish his entire agency, then besides getting his own salary for the rest of his life—and all agency employees getting theirs—the heroic administrator would also get a bonus of 10 percent of the agency's budget for five years. And what if the administrator can't find a way to make his agency unnecessary? Prescribes Buchwald, "If they're too dumb *not* to figure out how to take advantage of the reduction incentive plan, then they can keep working until they do."

Despite its compelling logic, we have not exactly embarked on the Buchwald Plan at Lexington or any other plant, and we're not fixing to try. But we have mounted a major attack on unnecessary paperwork—and paperwork jobs. And the more successful we are at it, the more opportunities we discover for further work-cutting and cost-cutting. Our campaign —called the Simplified Business Program (SBP)—has already produced huge savings, and we are beginning to realize that we have just begun to scratch the surface of opportunity.

Here is a bit of history, no doubt paralleled in some form by every large business, that forced us to take a hard look at our paperwork:

As indicated earlier, between 1956, when we moved to Lexington, and 1967, the cost of building typebar typewriters (total cost, including all attributable overhead) had been cut nearly in half. That was a proud and remarkable accomplishment—but unfortunately it was not to last. If our 1956 cost is taken as 100, and 1967 as 55, by 1973 the cost had reversed itself and crept up to an index of 75. At that rate all our gain would soon be wiped out.

Was this because of labor cost? True, labor cost had risen between 1967 and 1973, but by no means that sharply. Cost of materials? Parts and supplies were increasing in cost rather steadily at 2 percent a year, but some of that rise had been offset by changes in the product, in manufacturing methods, and in careful purchasing. That left overhead. We found that the biggest rise by far was the soaring cost of overhead. From 1956 to 1973, *indirect* costs of making a typewriter (all costs other than direct labor and parts) had risen 191 percent.

Sixty to 70 percent of the cost of overhead is the cost of indirect people. For every direct producer at Lexington, we now had one indirect person—doing accounting, personnel work, purchasing, production control, data processing, management, plant service, and so on. We call this an indirect-to-direct ratio of 1:1. Since indirect people on the average are paid more than directs, the dollar ratio is weighted on the side of indirect cost. The need for so many people is largely caused by formalized procedures. Procedures are the religion of bureaucracy.

It is a strange industrial phenomenon that making a procedure more complicated seldom requires approval from above —and when it does, the complication is generally received with favor. To simplify a procedure, however, requires many approvals and sign-offs, and proposing it usually carries considerable risk for the proposer. That is why procedure manuals grow into volumes. Our manual for purchasing alone fills two volumes, even though its essential substance could be boiled down to two pages.*

When we compared our indirect-to-direct ratio against that of some sister IBM plants, our 1:1 ratio didn't look bad at all. Plants making more sophisticated machines, such as com-

---

* Some companies are making major attacks on procedures, as we have been. One leader I know of, the Dana Corporation, reduced a volume of procedures down to a folded, pocket-size card.

Record Keeping

puters, often had less favorable ratios. But among our suppliers, most of them small businesses, we found ratios of only one indirect for as many as 15 to 20 directs. That's what troubled us. The alarming rise in our overhead cost appeared directly associated with bigness. Having slashed the cost—the *direct* cost—of building a typewriter, we were drowning ourselves in the cost of filling out pieces of paper that supposedly helped us keep track of the typewriters we were building.

An operator of a small machine shop wouldn't tolerate all that paperwork. If he didn't keep his own records, his wife or a hired bookkeeper would. Instead of squandering his revenue on a recorded history of every half-cent nut and bolt, he would want his accountant to tell him a few simple things: Did this order make money or not? Did he show a profit or a loss this year?

How could we, as a big producer (which theoretically should mean efficiency), restore the low-overhead efficiency of a small business? In analyzing why our business was growing so costly compared to a small machine shop, we discovered three basic principles that accounted for the difference:

1. While a small business operates as the total responsibility of the owner-manager, a big business such as ours operates on elaborate checks and balances among managers and functional departments, such as purchasing, engineering, and production control. These checks and balances generate tens of thousands of pieces of paper—to be prepared, circulated, computerized, accounted for, and filed.

2. Large organizations give rise to breeder departments, which we also call "cost generators." Certain functions not only are themselves costly and growing, but breed or generate costly work in other departments, as will soon be illustrated.

3. The 85–15 principle. In inventory control, which breeds immense amounts of paperwork, about 85 percent of the data concerns materials representing only 15 percent of inventory value. Conversely, about 15 percent of the data concerns 85 percent of inventory value. Yet the expense of accounting and

inventory control was spread equally over our tens of thousands of part numbers. It often cost as much to order, receive, check in, record the history of, and check out a half-cent nut and bolt as a precious item worth ten dollars.

Regarding the first principle, we were already making great strides in substituting total responsibility for unnecessary checks and balances. The payoff was already visible, and we were confident it would grow.

As for the second, we determined to identify, scrutinize, and start controlling breeder departments. One example of a breeder department, or cost generator, was our typebar type-design department. We had two or three talented type-design artists whose job it was to keep turning out new type styles as requested by sales planning. We had prided ourselves on offering customers a wide variety of typefaces—romans, sans serifs, italics, scripts, all in profuse variations. As long as those artists were there, they'd keep turning out new varieties because that's what they were paid to do.

The salaries of the artists were minor compared to the costs they generated. Each new type style meant engraving dies for a whole new alphabet, followed by tool engineering, manufacturing engineering, materials procurement, production control, quality assurance, type manufacturing, marketing, ever increasing complications for typewriter assembly, consignment of inventory, and a new stock number for order filling. One of our first ventures in simplified business procedures was to abolish the typebar type-design department.

On the same principle—but an illustration more applicable to other industries—we have reduced our department of production engineers who made engineering changes in the typebar typewriter. As long as there was a department charged with redesigning parts, they kept on redesigning parts. Each new change generates work in the toolroom, in purchasing, in production control, etc., etc. Also, what the engineer may not consider—it's not his job to consider it—is that there are hundreds of thousands of typewriters in customers' hands

which require the old part, and 180 branch offices stocked
with replacements for the old part. So he hasn't replaced a
part number, he's *added* one—with its own stock zone, another line on the inventory sheet, another item for the stock
men to count and the accountants to account for. This is not
to mention new instructions and a catalogue sheet for 5,000
customer engineers.

Our SBP solution: For mature products, reduce the production engineering department to a size adequate for handling
problems of quality and for redesigning parts when the new
design means a *major* cost reduction.

Quality control, when operated as a function divorced from
manufacture itself, can be a powerful cost generator. In our
Office Products Division, we pointedly did *not* have a quality
control manager. A quality controller at plant level, we discovered early in the game, can only do one thing efficiently:
He can demand reports. There is no way he can take responsibility for quality. That responsibility can only be carried
by the man or woman on the production line who does the
work, and his or her first-line manager. Quality control as
such can only sort the bad from the good (*if* it can detect the
defect).

Another cost generator is the plant layout department.
Over the years, we have spent as much as a million dollars
annually re-laying out our plant's equipment. As long as we
have a layout department, they'll keep re-laying out the plant.
We finally discovered—through our SBP campaign—that the
best way to reduce the cost of re-laying out the plant was to
reduce the size of the layout department.

Finally, the most stubborn cost generator in almost any
large company is headquarters. I used to keep telling our
headquarters that every time it added one person to its staff,
every plant throughout IBM had to add at least two people.
That headquarters person has got to *do* something, and if he's
to do anything he'll have to get some reports. He has to obtain
information, then has to disseminate it—and we'll have to

read it, so we'll be able to respond to it, so he'll have more stuff to disseminate, etc., etc. Sad to say, staffs, which periodically go through the obligatory routine of telling us we have to cut costs, are the most troublesome cost generators in industry.

So much for breeder departments and cost generators. The next chapter will deal with the 85–15 principle, which we discovered had all sorts of unexpected ramifications for simplifying our business procedures.

SIMPLIFIED
BUSINESS PROCEDURES
THE 85-15 PRINCIPLE

That soaring 191 percent rise in overhead expense forced us into a major self-evaluation. Were we to learn to live with this rising flood of paperwork? Or were we to try to recapture at least some of the simple efficiencies of the owner-managed machine shop?

I became convinced that simplified business procedures were possible—and necessary. In late 1971 at São Paulo, Brazil, at a meeting of our worldwide plant managers, we plotted a war on unnecessary paperwork. The summary statement of that meeting said in part:

The philosophy includes eliminating and simplifying procedures, files, paperwork and controls by increasing the responsibilities of individuals at all levels, direct and indirect. Where possible, entire functions as traditionally organized should be eliminated. Only enough controls and reports should be retained to protect the company assets. . . .

The timing of our meeting was propitious, for it coincided exactly with a series of forceful management letters by the chairman of our board to all IBM plants and offices on the dangers of bureaucracy and its growing cost.

In this war on paperwork, our first attack was against inventory controls. Trying to control the immensity of inventory was like trying to ride a runaway bronco. Who was really in control—the beast or the rider? The office products we produced at Lexington, for example, required that we list 80,000 part numbers. Every month our computer spilled out an inventory report, 50 part numbers to a page. The pages mounted to a monstrous pile of 1,600 sheets. A roomful of analysts scrutinized those 80,000 lines, one by one. If the computer printout signaled an alert to reorder a part, an analyst "analyzed" the alert, estimated how many more of those parts we would need in the short-run future, authorized a reorder, and then recomputed the change in our inventory.

Was all this necessary for all those parts? Our accountants advised that we mustn't tamper with the system. After all, their job was to account for everything.

Beautiful accounting can be tyrannical. And accounting is not as precise a science as many would have us believe. No matter how precisely we keep records, we still have shortages and overages of parts. When there's an inventory shortage, it's called a "loss"—an implication that the parts disappeared through theft or a big hole in the floor. When these "losses" are investigated, more often than not the shortage is not a disappearance of parts but an error in records.

Upon returning from São Paulo to Lexintgon, we instructed our computer to give us a special printout of our inventory—

in descending order of the value of the part numbers. And we confirmed a major suspicion. The first 190 pages of the list—12 percent of the part numbers—comprised 88 percent of our total inventory value. Conversely, of course, the remaining 1,410 pages (88 percent of the part numbers) added up to only 12 percent of our inventory value. Yet we were spending as much to "account" for washers and screws and nuts and bolts as for expensive power frames. This didn't make sense to us.

We decided that what we used to do for *all* our inventory we would now do only for the high-value 12 percent of part numbers. For these the computer would continue to alert us of dwindling stock; the analysts would estimate future needs and reorder. But for the remaining 88 percent, we clearly should try to simplify the procedures for control and reordering. Hereafter we would order many of the low-cost parts in amounts that would fill our needs for five years.

A five-year supply? What if a part number is obsoleted during the five-year period? What a waste!

We looked into that possibility—and found that the paperwork offered a far greater risk of wasteful expense than did scrapping the parts themselves. The most we could lose through obsoleting any part number in this low-cost category was only $100! Even that small figure was exaggerated, because we knew from experience that when a typewriter part is obsoleted, in almost all cases it must be retained in inventory by our branch offices for servicing typewriters already in customers' hands. We call that our "field-service inventory."

The simple five-year-supply system required one safeguard, however. Certain small parts, less standard than screws and washers, might require considerable time to resupply if, by some happenstance, we did run out. To forestall that possibility, we devised what we call the "bag" system. At the bottom of any bin of such parts, a minimum supply was packaged in small bags instead of lying loose. A bag was not to be

opened until all the loose supply was used up. Whoever opened
the first bag would have the responsibility—the total responsibility—of making sure a new supply was laid in. The quantities in these reserve bags assured ample time for reordering
a regular long-term supply.

This simple system was pioneered in our Austin and Berlin
plants and has worked extremely smoothly. We know that
the savings in people's time and in data processing work have
been considerable. We have a substantial clue as to how much
from having surveyed one part of the saving—in our field-
service inventory in Lexington.

The field-service inventory is made up of 30,000 part numbers, many of which have been obsoleted by engineering
changes in the typewriter. We are required by customer contracts to keep our branch offices supplied with these parts for
the servicing of older machines in customers' hands. As in our
manufacturing inventory, 85 percent of these parts were de-
controlled—more than 25,000 part numbers. That single stroke
cut in half—from ten to five—the staff of analysts who control
the field-service inventory. In addition to the salary saving,
the yearly load on our data processing department was reduced
by 360,000 sheets of paper.

Does that elimination of jobs conflict with our practice of
full employment? Not at all. Those able analysts were retrained and reassigned to new work, at their former pay level
or higher. Even during slack periods when the company is
required to establish a freeze on new hiring, job openings
frequently occur through normal attrition. The practice of
full employment is an assurance that the elimination of un-
productive jobs does not threaten one's personal job security
—and, in fact, provides an opportunity to make a more productive contribution.

At the time of our São Paulo meeting and the birth of SBP,
we were especially worried about our Berlin plant. Berlin
produced typebar typewriters for our European, African, and

Middle Eastern markets—the same markets for which Amsterdam was producing Selectrics. The rapidly rising popularity of the Selectric was causing some decline in the demand for the typebar machines. Furthermore, Berlin had an unfavorable ratio of 1.36 indirects to 1 direct, and the ratio threatened to get worse. The profitability of the plant was in serious jeopardy, so, in traditional industrial fashion, the Berlin management had kept adding indirect "problem solvers" to try to get costs down. The more they did so, the more indirect costs went up. Berlin, determined to end this vicious cycle, eagerly became our main laboratory for trying out new kinds of simplified business procedures.

The Berlin plant was among the first to decentralize parts inventory, shifting control from a warehouse area to the assembly line, and to embrace the 85–15 concept of decontrolling low-cost parts. Also, because the typebar typewriter was a mature product, Berlin virtually eliminated the processing of engineering changes and reassigned most of the people in the production engineering department. The success of these simplifications—and finding that the roof did not fall in as a result—led to more ideas, more experiments, and additional successes in other plants as well as Berlin:

1. Amsterdam greatly simplified the cost accounting of a major part of the Selectric, the power frame. This is the part for which we had installed the expensive transfer machine, described earlier. A major job in itself had been determining the manufacturing expense rate per hour of this million-dollar machine. In addition, we had followed the normal procedure of calculating direct labor claims for each of the operators in order to apply direct labor costs plus manufacturing expense to these claims.

Under their new SBP system, the Amsterdam people simply charged into one account *all* expenses of the operation—including direct labor, depreciation of the transfer machine, its maintenance, lubricants, square-footage space costs allocated to the department, and so on. Every month, they simply di-

vided this *total* figure by the number of power frames produced on all shifts. That gave them their unit cost. No labor
claims, no complex computations—yet they wound up with a
thoroughly adequate cost figure. The Amsterdam people estimate that they saved the work of two indirect people, mostly
through this change.

Needless to say, this new system of eliminating time claiming is appropriate only for the manufacture of established
products. To determine ''planned hours'' for a new product,
time claiming will probably be useful until the learning curve
of the production group levels off.

2. Our Berlin plant has adopted a modified version of the
above across-the-board accounting system, with good results
and again with a major saving in indirect people and other
expenses.

As a natural followup, the Berlin people looked at other
cost calculations, indirect as well as direct. They gave particular attention to simplification of their expense planning
and controls and reduction of the number of accounts and
cost centers.

3. The foregoing saving in paperwork and indirect cost led
to still another. A major annual undertaking of management,
from the bottom to the top levels of management, was preparation of the annual operating plan—the full-scale projection of
production, resources, personnel, space, unit costs, and so
forth. In short, the plan was a detailed road map of the year
ahead. But did it have to be *that* detailed?

Questioning the utility of the operating plan line by line, the
Berlin people reduced the old operating plan's 960 lines of
data down to 480 lines, exactly in half. The impact of this
saving was felt in every department.

4. Berlin made its biggest single saving through a simplification of inventory control. Normally, parts inventory falls
into two categories: (1) parts in stock, and (2) parts in work
process in machining and assembly departments. Berlin combined these inventory accounts. Under the new SBP system,

when parts and raw materials are received from vendors, they are checked into plant inventory. Then, no further control records are kept for minor parts until finished typewriters are checked out of final assembly. In this final checkout, the computer, having "memorized" exactly what parts and raw materials are contained in the specifications of each typewriter, automatically deducts those parts and materials from the plant inventory.

This inventory simplification enabled assignment of fully 25 percent of Berlin's stockroom people to other, more productive work. Many of them were placed in new jobs as direct producers, thus helping reverse the indirect-to-direct ratio.

5. Our plant in Boigny, France, has experimented successfully with a simplified system of entering all receiving procedures on a single card—eliminating many steps of error-prone paperwork between departments for purchasing, receiving, receiving inspection, and accounts payable. A purchasing department buyer and an accounts-payable person have been physically relocated to the plant receiving area. For every purchase order, the buyer prepares a single master card. When the parts or materials for that order arrive at the dock, the receiving department records the arrival on the card. The receiving inspector's report is entered on the same card. Let's say, hypothetically, that the shipment is of 100,000 parts; the inspector accepts 87,000 of them, rejecting and returning 13,-000. That is noted on the card. The accounts-payable person pays for the 87,000 parts, noting that fact on the same card.

This simple procedure not only is neat, orderly, and economical in itself, but eliminates the previous need for one department to communicate information to another department, each transfer bearing a potential for error. For example, if a purchase order for Part No. 789785 has two of those digits transposed in one of those communications—to No. 789875—a costly and confusing search and correction must be undertaken to straighten out a mixup all the way down the line. Besides reducing paper flow and saving manpower, the single-card system virtually eliminates the possibility of that kind of error.

6. In all our plants, we started taking a hard look at our computer programs, which largely had been developed from pre-computer functions with all their overly elaborated ''control'' procedures and data. Like many of IBM's computer customers, we, too, had to learn that a computer must not just absorb old systems, but is best used to revolutionize systems. Instead of just mechanizing the pencil, the object is to eliminate unnecessary functions, to simplify procedures, to define and fix people's responsibilities—then computerize the necessary procedures that remain. As an example of what not to do, one of our monthly computer printouts was a production control report that stretched 8.2 miles long. That much data is far more confusing than useful.

As a result of the SBP innovations, the Berlin plant has led all our Office Products plants in reversing the ratio of indirect personnel to directs. Starting from the December 1971 ratio of 1.36:1, by December 1972 the plant had tipped the balance to 0.82:1 and by December 1973 had attained a ratio of 0.68:1.

In the foreseeable future, the goal of increased productivity requires reduction of the *indirect* costs of manufacturing. That is where costs have most precipitously gone up and where they must be made to come down.

I am convinced that another major way to bring that cost down is to break down the distinction between indirect people and direct people. Traditionally, a person in a blue collar job stays stuck in that blue collar. White collar work stays pure white. That is inefficient and doesn't make sense. When a blue collar person is caught not having enough work to do, management usually has no trouble finding additional work to load on him. For some reason, waste of a blue collar person's time is considered an industrial crime. Yet while the white collar person's time usually costs more, it is so often squandered. If there's a little more white collar work than one person can do, a company thinks less of hiring a second person to take on the overload, even though it may not be an eight-hour-a-day requirement.

Why can't a blue collar person take on that overload? We've done it—in Berlin, in Lexington, and elsewhere—and it works. We have assemblers now spending two or three hours a day on indirect tasks related to their direct work, such as stock control of parts with which their assembly work has made them familiar. They welcome the change. The increased sense of responsibility seems to benefit both jobs. In Boigny, France, several groups have taken over many indirect responsibilities with no loss of production. An important reason indirect costs have risen so sharply is that many indirect people have insufficiently large assignments—and the best way to avoid that problem is to combine indirect and direct work.

14

DEPARTMENTAL WORKSHOPS

The idea of creative workshops on a small, departmental scale was so simple that at first we didn't know what to name the project. So, until we could think of a name, we called it Program III (our first workshop having been Work Simplification; the second, Workmanship Analysis).

Program III was different from its two predecessors, however. They were aimed at training for specific skills: (1) the skill of time-and-motion engineering, and (2) the skill of analyzing and mastering quality. Program III aimed at problem *identification* and problem solving on the broadest scale.

On the basic assumption which underlies everything we do—
the assumption that the person who does the work knows the
work best—we hoped to evoke, capture, and implement the
accumulated experience and wisdom of everyone in our plants
to help make our work more productive.

Note the emphasis on *identifying* problems as well as attacking them. While we managers may regard ourselves as skilled
in attacking problems, we don't always attack the right ones.
The people who do the work are uniquely able to identify
problems that may never occur to management—and sometimes these are the most important problems.

Unlike Work Simplification and Workmanship Analysis,
Program III is *not* a training program. It is a creativity
program. It is an organized way to release people's urges to
improve the workplace. The object is to lift the lid from the
boiling pot of ideas that bubble in the mind of every inteHigent
person who works on a job day in and day out, who feels
frustrations at poor methods, and who craves the satisfaction
of helping improve methods. Every group of experienced and
intelligent people, almost any department in any plant, vi-
brates, almost bursts, with perceptions and ideas for improvement. But the industrial tradition is to seal the lid against
all that valuable insight. Don't let any of the ideas out—and
don't let any information in that might encourage ideas. In
short, keep people's *hands* busy—and hope that their minds
idle in neutral, lest someone come up with a dangerous thought.

The only "training" that takes place in departmental workshops—that's how we informally began defining Program III
until we decided formally to call it just that, Departmental
Workshops—is accomplished in ten minutes or so: enough
time to explain how the well-known method of *brainstorming*
works. From there on, it's all creativity.

At this writing, departmental workshops are still new in
our plants. Different plants put them to different uses in
different ways. The discovery of their full potential still lies

ahead. But from our first trial run, every departmental-work-shop series has exploded with workable and productive ideas. Nothing we have ever done has so infused departments with a commonness of purpose, a team urge to accomplish and improve, a sense of participating in a company. The power of this creativity-releasing experience is in its directness and simplicity.

Like most successful ideas, departmental workshops were inspired not by a bolt from the blue but by sheer need. Early in the 1970s a new set of problems emerged at Lexington. Our site had grown very large, to a population of about 6,000. Further expansion would be inefficient to manage—in fact, I sometimes wished we had not permitted it to grow that large. The enormous success of the Selectric and the continued demand for our traditional typebar typewriter (which had not declined as we had anticipated) were straining our production capacity. We had to move other products—first the dictating equipment, then the Copier—to other plants. Also, during this period a national business downturn required a companywide slowdown on new hiring.

The coupling of these events—the temporary job freeze in the plant and the narrowing of our plant product lines—visibly shrank promotional opportunities for our people. Since our system of motivation was largely based on career advancement as an important reward, it was no great surprise that morale surveys began to reflect a drop in enthusiasm. We needed some new way to ignite the eagerness of our people to stretch toward new goals, in the way that our Work Simplification and Workmanship Analysis courses had done so effectively in the previous decade. To reinstitute those courses, even as refreshers, would not do. They had already accomplished their purpose so well—and the turnover of our people had been so small—that a "warmover" of old projects would have been redundant.

Our success had always been based on involving our people

in solving problems, for the benefit of all concerned. How could we now continue and expand that profitable partnership? One day the simple thought occurred to us: Why not have our people tell *us* what stumbling blocks to higher productivity most frustrated them—and why not enlist *their* wisdom to remove these stumbling blocks?

We soon mapped out a simple, three-session project—that is, three sessions just as a starter. Unlike the two previous plant-wide projects, these sessions were not to be random mixes of managers and operators from diverse departments. These would be meetings of each department, in which people, led by their own department manager, would closely examine their own departmental goals and get everyone involved in achieving them. Thus the meetings would be team solidifiers—even a form of competition between departmental teams.

To create a maximum feeling of trust and cooperation, we decided that in the first meeting of the series we would *give* before asking to *receive*. We would explain the company's situation more openly and frankly than our company—and, I dare say, any company of comparable size—had ever done before.

SESSION 1

To open with a sense of relaxation, a department of 20 people or so gathers for breakfast at a local motel. To emphasize the importance of the meeting, their first speaker is either the product manager or the plant manager. The speaker tells them they are there because the company wants to benefit from their experience and thought, but that first he wishes to tell them some things about IBM.

He starts off by reporting on the state of the company: its gross income, costs, taxes, net earnings, earnings per share of stock, total worth, long-term debt, and so on. (These figures are already in the public domain, appearing in the report to stockholders.) Then, emphasizing the audience's responsibility to keep data confidential, he presents information about their division, their plant, and their department that no one on the outside is permitted to know. This includes, first, a fairly detailed breakdown of the Office Products Division in the form of a pie chart, showing in percentages how revenue is divided —into product costs, marketing expense, warranty cost, administration, product development, taxes, etc., and net profit. Then further information on the Lexington plant: its growth in space, manpower, and production; and most important for the purposes of this meeting, the buildup of the backlog of unfulfilled orders, product by product. This customer backlog is then translated into its revenue impact—the tens of millions of dollars that the Lexington plant alone could additionally produce if its people found ways to catch up on that backlog.

The audience is shown how previous productivity campaigns produced remarkable results which now have leveled off; how rising wages, employee benefits, overhead, and cost of materials now demand new ingenuity to increase efficiency; and how the plant's suggestion activities are continuing in high gear but everyone's ideas are needed more than ever. The speaker then leads a general discussion and answers questions for as long as people keep asking them. In his answers, he particularly emphasizes that productivity growth has always brought higher pay levels, better promotional opportunities, and more awards—as well as personal satisfactions—and that rather than threatening job security, productivity growth provides the financial wherewithal for maintaining full employment.

For the remainder of the two- to three-hour session, the department manager explains how at the next session the members will be asked to brainstorm ideas for breaking bottlenecks and eliminating inefficiencies. He explains carefully how brainstorming works: Members will be asked to fire off ideas in a totally positive and encouraging atmosphere. That means no negative or discouraging comments of any kind and no derisive laughter, no matter how far out the idea. Every five or ten minutes—as soon as the group seems to run out of gas on a particular topic—the manager will introduce a new problem area on which suggestions are needed. The group should shoot for *quantity* of ideas, not quality. The recorded ideas will be screened for quality later, and the group itself will participate at the third session in choosing the most practical or most promising ideas, and help decide which ones ought to be implemented first.

SESSION 2

At this session, which takes place three days or so after the first one, the department manager reviews the rules of brainstorming. He announces the topics to be brainstormed and chooses a recorder, who jots down the ideas on an easel.

One of the amazing things—even to those of us who were most optimistic about this venture—is the sheer quantity of ideas that start pouring forth, many from individuals considered the most shy or least creative. Two-hour sessions by single departments have produced recorded ideas ranging in number from 100 to more than 300, generated by six to ten topic areas. For example, a department devoted to the stocking and physical handling of parts had as one of their problem topics ''better utilization of space.'' Here is a verbatim list of the ideas jotted down by the recorder. Most are self-explanatory.

Package more parts
Better vendor containers
Better-made boxes
More parts on skids
Stack higher
Consolidate parts on skids
Stack pallets
Uniform skids
Palletize stock
Standard pallets
Larger world-trade blankets
Larger vendor 689
Fewer work stations
More manpower
Stockroom closer to lines
Move department drop areas
Combine B.O. bench with file

Narrow aisles
Smaller bins—small parts zone
Short distance
Taller shelves
Scrap obsolete parts
Reduce inventory levels
More parts on line (assembly and others)
Larger line blanket quantities
Automation of issuing parts
Use all plastic bags
Update package parts listing
Better system for ordering parts
Roof storage

Extend racks
Terminate receiving and inspection areas
Faster trucks (new fork trucks)
Even flow of parts
Put parts on right location
Automation of parts storage
Basement storage
Outside storage
Transfer parts
Underground stockroom
Wholesale parts zones
Rotation of stock
Total vendor assembly

Once stimulated by the buoyancy of the brainstorming session, members often think of additional ideas later. They are encouraged to go to their manager's office any time after the session to add to the list, which he posts on his wall. Soon after the session the manager prints and distributes the list of ideas for all members of his department. In doing so, he may eliminate near duplications and those ideas that are obviously far-out and impractical.

SESSION 3

This session may take place a week or so after the brainstorming session. Now is the time for department members to evaluate ideas on the list. Each person is asked to rank the ideas. As a guide to ranking, the manager might ask, ''Which of these ideas would be best to start working on in the next five days?''

The manager might simply count the number of votes for each idea. Eliminating those with few votes or none, he takes a new tally until a consensus on one ''most urgent'' idea, or possibly two or three ideas, is achieved. If the manager believes that achievement of the idea is, for any reason, not feasible, he is expected to say so and argue his viewpoint right then and there. Otherwise, his people will expect him to lead them in achieving it.

Also, he should assure his people that only one, two, or three ideas were chosen so that the department could concentrate its efforts. Additional good ideas will be placed on future agendas.

As an example of priority-setting, the parts handling department chose the best ideas on its list and ranked them as follows:

1. Package more parts
2. Better vendor containers
3. Uniform skids
4. Scrap obsolete parts
5. More parts on line (assembly & others)
6. Larger line blanket quantities
7. Larger vendor 689
8. More manpower
9. Stockroom closer to lines
10. Even flow of parts
11. Better system for ordering parts
12. Rotation of stock
13. Total vendor assembly

In the Toronto plant, a department of engineers was surprised at the similarity between many of its ideas and those of assembly department workshops. According to the Toronto plant manager, when an engineering change in assembly was required, the engineers began asking whether the assemblers had come up with any ideas in their workshops. No wonder. In one workshop, an operator suggested eliminating a certain heat-treating specification, saying it was unnecessary. Engineers, checking it out, found the man was absolutely right. The department force was thus reduced by one man (and the man who made the suggestion was rewarded). That suggestion paid for the workshop more than ten times over in a single year.

Another Toronto workshop came up with a specific innovation that no M.I.T.-trained engineer or Harvard-trained manager would be likely to think of—yet it broke a bottleneck. Women in the department complained that work was seriously delayed—and nerves frazzled—because women had to line up waiting to use ladies'-room sinks. How about more sinks? This sparked another idea: The problem was not sinks. The lines ~~Mirrors~~ were caused by women using the mirrors that hung over the sinks. Why not move the mirrors to the opposite wall? The idea was tried—and the problem was solved!

That idea was entirely unexpected. It came as an offshoot of some "problem topic" proposed by the manager. This points up a controversy among the enthusiastic supporters of departmental workshops. Some managers believe the workshops should be as open-ended and unstructured as possible, to invite such surprise ideas. Others believe topics should be carefully chosen and discussion focused to dig deeply into a troublesome problem, even if at the loss of occasional unexpected dividends. The people in our Bogotá plant, for example, have come to the latter conclusion. As evidence, they point out that recently, upon taking on a new product, they cut learning-curve time to half of what it had been for a previous new product. They attribute the remarkable improvement to concentrated brainstorming in departmental workshops.

Different plants—in fact, different managers—will resolve this controversy in different ways, with some going one way, some the other, and some a combination of both. Perhaps long experience will eventually point to an optimal method. The important thing is to try everything, keep an open mind, and decide through experience rather than theory.

Within a maximum of four weeks following that third (or evaluation-and-action) session, a review session must be called. In this review the manager reports progress in implementing the department's ideas. This review session, besides maintaining the feeling of creativity and accomplishment, has two important byproducts.

First, such review sessions can go on periodically—forever.

Thus, departmental workshops, unlike work simplification and workmanship analysis, are a long-range, continuing device for keeping people aware that productivity improvement is a never-ending goal. The solution of every problem opens opportunities to identify and solve new problems.

Second, these followup sessions are a welcome replacement for old forms of departmental meetings. Before the advent of departmental workshops, it was our policy that managers had to have periodic department meetings, if for no other reason than to maintain communication between a manager and his people. In theory that was fine, but it seldom accomplished much of substance. Obligated to run a meeting, the manager would prepare a chart and give a speech—or invite some functional specialist from elsewhere in the plant to give a talk.

Our attitude surveys revealed that people held a low opinion of most of these meetings. Curious as to why, I and a couple of other top managers ran our own simple survey by asking some people at random what was wrong with those meetings. Almost invariably, the answer was, "They're a waste of time." That answer always fascinated me. According to the widespread myth about employee attitudes, they should be delighted to leave their workbenches and sit in a comfortable chair listening to some speaker drone on—at company expense. But the truth is people resent having their time wasted. They dislike just listening and not participating, not making a constructive contribution.

This "survey" confirmed my basic belief that people want their company to succeed—and want to help make it succeed, if they're just given the chance. That belief is further confirmed by anonymous comments written by department members at the end of one departmental workshop:

"I liked the idea real well because it gave you an idea of how the company was going, where we needed improvement. Also shows we need to hire more people, so this shows the employee that he has good job security."

"I think this [Session 2] was better than Session 1 because it let everyone think more and come up with his or her ideas on different questions. Also I think the idea of competition [between departments] made it better. Also you get a lot of good ideas this way."

"Very informing. It gave me a better idea of the company as a whole. Brings all employees closer together. Gave me the incentive to work harder. Gave me an idea of how the company is doing against its competition."

"Both sessions were most informing. Enjoyed second session a lot, brainstorming ideas. I think overall program will help all departments in plant."

"Should do this more often."

"I feel sessions one and two were informative, especially session one. I learned quite a few things of which I had no ideas. It gave me more of an insight into how big and complex the business really is. I also feel a lot of worthwhile ideas should come from the brainstorming session."

"The past two meetings have made me start thinking in terms of IBM policy and reflection of the company on how to benefit myself and the company for a better company."

"If we continue to communicate in the way we started, then our company will be a better place to work."

One department manager summed up his experience: "At most of my regular department meetings, assembly people would either say nothing at all or else mutter, 'What's in it for me?' or 'What are you doing for me?' Seldom would they voice interest or say 'thank you.' I personally think it's money well spent to put this type of program on. The employees now want to know what's going on . . . and I think they have a right to know."

There's no doubt in my mind that most old-line, dollars-and-cents, nose-to-the-grindstone managers will demand proof that this radical venture has a measurable payoff. I have no proof that will satisfy them. It may be years until proof is available —if the payoff can ever be measured. My reply is reason and common sense rather than proof. Twenty workshop hours (three original meetings plus two or three followups) is about 1 percent of a person's working year. Based on the spectacular success of work simplification and workmanship analysis —all measured—and the already heartening improvements brought about by early, experimental departmental workshops, it seems unreasonable to me that we will gain less than a 3–5 percent increase in efficiency. I predict the gain will be even more.

But even disregarding that, the payoff in morale is easily worth the price. What better way can there be to help a big business operate with the intimacy and efficiency of a small one than to give every person in it a chance to contribute a good idea?

A most important side benefit of departmental workshops is that they give us an opportunity, a better one than we have ever had before, to learn how effective our managers really are —how well they communicate with their people, how well they are accepted as leaders, and how effective they are at followup. The whole department will be watching how the manager pushes forward the ideas that they created and he accepted. When he does well, his leadership will be enhanced. On the other hand, if he falters in the critical stage of followup, that's something *his* managers need to know.

Because the success of departmental workshops is so dependent on the manager's effectiveness, we enrolled every manager in a course to prepare for the workshops—developing skills that ought to strengthen him not only in the workshops but in other areas as well. Chiefly, these are communications skills.

At the outset, our course was based on conventional approaches to public speaking, making presentations, and building self-confidence in dealing with individuals and groups. Almost unanimously, department managers expressed great satisfaction—feelings of enrichment and growth—from the course. Increasingly, however, we found this course inadequate for workshop needs. Making a manager a more effective speaker was all well and good, but in a sense it was just the opposite of the role he would best serve in a departmental workshop. His most important role there is as an *elicitor* of the thoughts of other people, who are often shy and unconfident. He should be an encourager, a stimulator, a person who can control enthusiasm without diminishing it. And—very important—he has to be a clarifier, a summarizer, and one who can bring down a curtain while leaving spirits at their highest.

These are skills which no one—at least no one we have been able to find—is presently teaching. So, as we did with workmanship analysis, we have had to set about creating our own course. Criticism of one another, criticism of self as seen on videotape, and a mutually supportive atmosphere (similar to that of brainstorming) form the basis of our emerging course. We find that some "students" are natural experts from whom the others learn.

Our early experiments in departmental workshops have convinced me that a generation or two from now, a student of business management will read a history of how industry was conducted during most of the twentieth century and will ask in disbelief: "You mean they had factories of 5,000 people who had combined working experience of, say, 50,000 years—and nobody ever took those people into their confidence and asked their advice?"

ON MANAGEMENT
AND MANAGERS

If everything in this book were to be summarized in a single sentence, that sentence would be: "Improve productivity by utilizing people's minds as well as their hands."

Most companies waste the talents of their managers as freely as they do the talents of their nonmanagerial people. Instead of using their minds creatively for true management, most managers are merely used as a "booster signal" to relay orders from the top. A manager should be freed to use his mind and to exercise his authority. Otherwise he will eventually become a counterproductive manager.

Most managers know this, but *their* top managers, while knowing it too, refuse to free them. Is that statement too heavy-handed and exaggerated? Not according to an extensive survey of management practice and management desire conducted by Rensis Likert, director of the Institute for Social Research of the University of Michigan. Likert and his staff devised a far-ranging and practical questionnaire to study the practices and desires of top- and middle-level managers in "several well-managed companies." He broke down the elements of management practice into four basic management styles, or systems. The results are summarized in Table 2. For full details of how the practices were broken down into these styles, the reader will profit by consulting Likert's book, *The Human Organization.*

As we scan the table, of course our reaction is more pleasant as our eyes move toward the right. The column to the extreme left, System 1, looks like a police state. The column to the right, System 4, looks like an ideal but (we somehow assume) nonexistent company.

Which column, or system, is associated with the highest productivity? Likert looked into that. He asked all the managers he surveyed to complete questionnaires concerning management practices in each department of their company. Likert analyzed the results and categorized each department of each company according to the management system that predominated there. In a separate effort, he asked the same managers to rate the *productivity* of each department, as high (h) or low (l).

And what did he find? Virtually without fail, *the greater the participation of managers*—down to the lowest level of managers—in responsibility, communication, decision making, and goal setting, *the higher the department's productivity.* As Professor Likert put it:

The striking fact . . . is that irrespective of where the h's describing the high-producing unit fall in the table, the l's for the low-

Table 2

SYSTEM 1: EXPLOITIVE— AUTHORITATIVE	SYSTEM 2: BENEVOLENT— AUTHORITATIVE	SYSTEM 3: CONSULTATIVE	SYSTEM 4: PARTICIPATIVE GROUP
Top management feels much responsibility; lower levels, less. Rank and file often hostile to company goals.	Top management and most middle-level managers feel responsibility. Rank and file feel relatively little.	Substantial proportion of personnel feel responsibility; generally try to achieve goals.	Personnel feel real responsibility; are motivated to achieve goals.
Subservient and hostile attitudes toward superiors, hostility toward peers, and contempt for subordinates. Widespread distrust.	Subservient attitudes toward superiors; condescension toward subordinates; and hostility toward peers, resulting from competition.	Reasonably cooperative attitudes, but with some competitive hostility toward peers and condescension toward subordinates.	Cooperative attitudes throughout, with mutual trust and confidence.
Very little communication; goals initiated at top and directed downward. Received with great suspicion.	Little communication; goals primarily come from top, or are patterned on communication from top. Directed mostly downward. Goals sometimes received with suspicion.	Communication on goals sometimes initiated at lower levels, but patterned on communication from top. Often accepted, but sometimes with suspicion.	Much communication among both individuals and groups. Communication is down, up, and with peers. Goals are initiated at all levels. Are generally accepted, or at least openly and candidly questioned.

Superiors and subordinates far apart in knowing and understanding one another's problems. Often perceive each other erroneously.	Superiors and subordinates moderately close if proper roles are kept; mutual perceptions in error on some points.	Superiors and subordinates fairly close. Mutual perceptions moderately accurate.	Superiors and subordinates usually very close. Mutual perceptions usually quite accurate.
Decisions usually made at top, based on partial, often inaccurate information regarding problems at lower levels. Decision usually inspires little motivation below.	Policy decided at top, but many implementations decided below. Implementation decisions based on moderately accurate and adequate information, but often made at levels higher than where best information exists.	Broad policy established at top; more specific decisions, lower. Decisions based on reasonably adequate information, although sometimes made higher than where best information exists.	Decisions made widely throughout company. Decisions well-integrated, based on information from all levels. Decisions generally pushed downward to where best information exists.
Goals pressed by top in the form of orders. Overtly accepted but covertly resisted strongly. Very strong pressure to meet goals, so strong tendency for people to distort and falsify measurements and reports.	Goals issued by top as orders but sometimes with opportunity to comment. Overtly accepted but often covertly resisted to a moderate extent. Fairly strong pressure to meet goals, so fairly strong tendency for people to distort and falsify measurements and reports.	Goals issued as orders after discussion of problems with subordinates. Overtly accepted but at times with covert resistance. Some pressure to protect self, hence to distort measurements and reports.	Goals established by group participation except in emergency. Lower levels sometimes press for higher goals. Goals fully accepted, both overtly and covertly. Strong pressure at all levels to obtain complete and accurate information, hence accurate measurements and reports.

producing department fall to the left. Quite consistently, the high-producing department is seen as toward the right end of the table. For the vast majority of managers, this has been the pattern for every item in the table, irrespective of the field of experience of the manager—production, sales, financial, office, etc.—and regardless of whether he occupies a staff or a line position. . . .

One would expect that such extraordinary consensus would lead managers to manage in ways consistent with it. . . . Why do managers use a system of management which they recognize is less productive than an alternate system which they can describe correctly and presumably could use? All these managers keenly want to achieve outstanding success. What keeps them from using the management system which they recognize yields the highest productivity, lowest costs, and best performance? *

Those are questions that have often puzzled me. Likert points out an even more puzzling phenomenon: "Most managers report that when top management seeks to reduce cost, it shifts its system more toward System 1, i.e., toward a system which they know from their own observations and experience yields poorer productivity and higher costs."

Two simple charts dramatize the contrast between what these managers *do* and what they say they would *like* to do. Figure 9 shows the distribution of answers to the first questionnaire (Form A). These answers indicate the managers' perception of how their companies actually operate. Their answers are scattered throughout the chart, among all four systems. Their center of gravity lies between System 2 and System 3.

Now compare that against Figure 10, what middle and top managers "would like to have." This figure charts the managers' responses to Form B, the second questionnaire. The results are almost a straight line, dead center under System 4.

Are these people too idealistic? Suppose management desire

---

* From The Human Organization, by Rensis Likert, Copyright 1967 by McGraw-Hill Book Company. Used with permission of McGraw-Hill Book Company.

Figure 9. Distribution of answers on Form A of middle- and upper-level managers in several well-managed companies.

Operating characteristics		System 1 Exploitive— authoritative	System 2 Benevolent— authoritative	System 3 Consultative	System 4 Participative group	Item no.
Motivations	1a*					1
	b					2
	c					3
	d					4
	e					5
	f					6
	g					7
Communication	2a					8
	b					9
	c(1)					10
	(2)					11
	d(1)					12
	(2)					13
	(3)					14
	(4)					15
	(5)					16
	e					17
	f					18
	(1)					19
Interaction	3a					20
	b					21
	c(1)					22
	(2)					23
	d					24
	e					25
Decision making	4a					26
	b					27
	c					28
	d					29
	e(1)					30
	(2)					31
	f					32
Goal setting	5a					33
	b					34
	c					35
Control	6a					36
	b					37
	c					38
	d					39
Performance	7a					40
	b					41
	c					42
	d					43

Total

* This column indicates the numbers and letters of the questionnaire items.

Source: Rensis Likert, The Human Organization. Copyright 1967 by McGraw-Hill Book Company. Used with permission of McGraw-Hill Book Company.

Figure 10. Profile of answers on Form B of middle- and upper-level managers in several well-managed companies, indicating the management system they would like to have.

Operating characteristics		System 1 Exploitive— authoritative	System 2 Benevolent— authoritative	System 3 Consultative	System 4 Participative group	Item no.
Motivations	1a					1
	b					2
	c					3
	d					4
	e					5
	f					6
	g					7
Communication	2a					8
	b					9
	c(1)					10
	(2)					11
	d(1)					12
	(2)					13
	(3)					14
	(4)					15
	(5)					16
	e					17
	f					18
	(1)					19
Interaction	3a					20
	b					21
	c(1)					22
	(2)					23
	d					24
	e					25
Decision making	4a					26
	b					27
	c					28
	d					29
	e(1)					30
	(2)					31
	f					32
Goal setting	5a					33
	b					34
	c					35
Control	6a					36
	b					37
	c					38
	d					39
Performance	7a					40
	b					41
	c					42
	d					43
Total						

Source: Rensis Likert, The Human Organization. Copyright 1967 by McGraw-Hill Book Company. Used with permission of McGraw-Hill Book Company.

and management practice merged, and moved all the way to the right—all the way to System 4. Is there any hard evidence that higher productivity would actually result?

Professor Likert singles out, in Figure 11, what he describes as an "extraordinarily productive plant." He charts how that plant's managers perceive their actual operations—not what they "would like to have," but what they *do* (at least, what they did in the mid-1960s, shortly before publication of *The Human Organization*). In this chart, which is strikingly similar to Figure 10, the answers fall almost entirely under System 4. This chart is important because it confirms that participative management and high productivity go hand in hand.

I must add that the chart confirms something else, at least to me. The chart records the answers of managers at our Lexington plant, during the time I was plant manager. What it confirms is that what we at the top were setting *as policy*—all the policies described heretofore in this book—were actually perceived *as practice* by managers throughout the organization. In other words, policy as conceived by top management had been successfully translated into practice.

Having thus summarized the relationship between participative management and productivity at Lexington, I would like to add some observations about the art of management that I've gleaned over the years, both as a manager and as a person managed.

A first-line manager (or foreman) has just one essential responsibility, and that is to manage 20 or so people—to create an atmosphere that will bring out everyone's best. If he does that skillfully, it will take his full eight hours a day and he shouldn't be distracted from it. We always instructed our new first-line managers: Don't worry about finance. Don't worry about your next production quota, or even if you're meeting the present one. If and when you fall behind, we'll tell you. Just tend to your people's needs so they can work well.

I used to say at the first indoctrination meeting of new

Figure 11. Management system used by the most productive plant of a well-managed company, as seen by managers in that plant.

Operating characteristics		System 1 Exploitive— authoritative	System 2 Benevolent— authoritative	System 3 Consultative	System 4 Participative group	Item no.
Motivations	1a					1
	b					2
	c					3
	d					4
	e					5
	f					6
	g					7
Communication	2a					8
	b					9
	c(1)					10
	(2)					11
	d(1)					12
	(2)					13
	(3)					14
	(4)					15
	(5)					16
	e					17
	f					18
	(1)					19
Interaction	3a					20
	b					21
	c(1)					22
	(2)					23
	d					24
	e					25
Decision making	4a					26
	b					27
	c					28
	d					29
	e(1)					30
	(2)					31
	f					32
Goal setting	5a					33
	b					34
	c					35
Control	6a					36
	b					37
	c					38
	d					39
Performance	7a					40
	b					41
	c					42
	d					43

Total

managers, just promoted from the workbench: "When you run into a problem, your first inclination will be to try to solve it—yourself—in a technical way. When you're a real manager, you'll find you don't think that way any more. Your first thought will be of your 20 people—which of them can grow most by solving this problem? If you decide it's beyond solving by your own people, you'll then ask yourself what person in your product group you can call to solve it—a product engineering person or manufacturing engineering person or whom? But if you keep thinking of how to solve that technical problem instead of worrying about those 20 people, you haven't yet made it as a manager."

What do I mean by "worrying about" those 20 people? First, are any of them feeling troubled or insecure in their work in some way that inhibits their best efforts? A manager who is "too busy" to worry about his people's feelings would be amazed to realize what those feelings may be—and how they probably involve *him*.

I clearly remember an assembly-line co-worker of mine, recently transferred from another job, who was unsure of himself in his new duties. On his first day on the new job, he acted nervous all day, making slips of the hand, and more and more things went wrong as the day wore on. Finally I asked if he was OK. He admitted, after some evasive mumbling, that our manager always said hello to him in the morning—but this morning he hadn't. It upset and worried him.

Was my co-worker being too sensitive? Maybe. But maybe our manager wasn't sensitive enough, especially toward a new person feeling his way in a new job. A problem may be that simple.

Years later, when I was plant manager, a man came to me to announce that he was sorry but he just *had* to quit. Why? Well, his mother had been in a hospital seriously ill, and he had asked for a couple of days off to sit with her. His manager had readily granted the request. Then what was the problem? "He *knew* my mother almost died—that's why I asked for the time. It's now two weeks I've been back, and he never once asked about my mother. If that's what this company means about concern for its employees, I'm leaving.'' Before we were through, the man cooled down and decided not to quit. But his anger was justified: His manager must have had his mind on solving some technical problem, not on his people.

Taking care of one's people means defending one's people— even when they may be wrong. How many times has any of us admired a baseball manager for running out to the umpire to protest a close call that went against his man? We know—*he* knows—that the umpire is not going to reverse the call, but the manager is showing his team that he cares as much as they do, that he's their strongest supporter. What a morale booster!

I remember, early in World War II, when I was assembling a device we produced for the Navy. I inadvertently allowed some goof to go through—several times—until the project manager himself came storming down. My first-line manager intervened, showing that the task was difficult, the error unimportant, anything to take the heat off me. As soon as the project manager turned the corner toward his office, my immediate boss turned to me with an entirely changed face and tone and demanded, ''Now, don't let that damn thing happen again.'' That's what makes a person willing to jump out the window for his manager.

Do these anecdotes seem small and frivolous? They are as fundamental to a management structure as pillars are to a bridge. The first-line manager is the personification of the whole management structure, of management policy, of what the company stands for in the eyes of the man or woman doing the work. He is the point of contact between the operator and the rest of the company. If the manager is mean and cold, the company is mean and cold; if he's considerate and supportive, the company is a good place to work. That is why nothing should distract a first-line manager from his first responsibility—looking after his people. When he does that, he can ask anything reasonable, and people will do anything reasonable for him.

To this day, I warmly remember the time my manager, during my early days, came to me late in the afternoon of the last day before a Christmas holiday to say there was one special machine we had to get out somehow that night. It meant staying a couple of extra hours. I felt good about his request, not because I got the job out, but because that man had helped me and defended me when I needed him, and now he was asking me a favor and had confidence that I'd do it.

The skills of a first-line manager are skills of personality and of experience in working with people. That is why a first-line manager should be promoted from the production line itself—where he learns through long experience the problems and viewpoints of the people he is asked to manage. And that is why he should be selected from a list of top producers—because top producers have already commanded the respect of their co-workers.

Needless to say, being a top producer does not automatically qualify a person as a manager, not by a long shot. But being a top producer is one qualification. As a next step, all eligible top producers must be judged on their potential for learning to meet the following characteristics of a good first-line manager:

1. He must be *completely people-oriented*. His success depends on what his people do. He should not be distracted at this point in his career by training in analyzing reports or any unusually complex paperwork.

2. He should *readily call on service groups* within his product group for technical assistance, financial assistance, any kind of special skill outside his chief responsibility of people-orientation.

3. He must be *easy to talk to,* and *reliable to talk to.* This means he must listen more than he talks—including listening

and watching for what a person may be trying to say but can't bring himself to state clearly. It means he must build a reputation for fairness, for consistency, and for keeping his promises. The most important tool in his managerial tool kit is earned trust.

4. To *his* managers, he must be accountable and held accountable for what happens in his department—particularly for morale, which flows naturally from points 1, 2, and 3.

Once he is promoted beyond first-line manager, we train him further—and expect more of him. At this point people-orientation, while always remaining important, becomes secondary to management of the systematic functioning of the organization. When I was plant manager, I rated product managers on four main points:

1. Schedules—developing and meeting them.
2. Cost—the maintenance and improvement of efficiency.
3. Quality maintenance.
4. Morale.

The last of these, morale, never diminishes in importance, regardless of the management level a person attains. A manager always remains accountable for morale, for that is the critical ingredient of productivity. I have never known a low-morale department to be efficient, nor a low-efficiency department to have high morale. Conversely, a high-morale department is almost always an efficient department.

To measure morale, we conducted a quarterly survey covering 25 percent of all the people in the plant—people in manufacturing, offices, warehouse and shipping, the cafeteria, managers, everybody. Thus, every individual was sounded out once a year. Each survey contained 15 to 40 questions, covering whatever attitude issues concerned us at that particular time.

Among these were six key questions which reappeared in every survey, and which in fact appeared in every morale survey throughout all the divisions of IBM. The questions and answers were:

1. *How would you rate IBM as a company to work for compared to other companies you know about?*
   (a) One of the best.   (b) Above average.   (c) Average.
   (d) Below average.   (e) One of the worst.
2. *How do you like your job—the kind of work you do?*
   (a) It's very good.   (b) Good.   (c) Average.   (d) Poor.
   (e) Very poor.
3. *How would you rate your salary considering your duties and responsibilities?*
   (a) Very good.   (b) Good.   (c) Average.   (d) Poor.
   (e) Very poor.
4. *How would you rate your opportunity to move into a better job in IBM?*
   (a) Very good.   (b) Good.   (c) Average.   (d) Poor.
   (e) Very poor.
5. *How good a job do you feel is being done by your immediate manager?*
   (a) Very good.   (b) Good.   (c) So-so.   (d) Poor.
   (e) Very poor.
6. *Considering everything, how would you rate your overall satisfaction in IBM at the present time?*
   (a) Completely satisfied.   (b) Very satisfied.   (c) Satisfied.
   (d) Neither satisfied nor dissatisfied.   (e) Dissatisfied.
   (f) Very dissatisfied.   (g) Completely dissatisfied.

Those constant questions permitted us to chart numerically (1) a history of trends in our own plant, and (2) a comparison against attitudes in other IBM plants. We combined answers (a) and (b) in our chart as favorable, answers (d) and (e) as negative, and answer (c) as neutral. For question 6, which had seven possible answers, we considered (a)–(c) favorable, (e)–(g) negative, and (d) neutral.

The morale survey is still our basic device for sensing shifts in attitude. It is supplemented by careful attention to "Speak Up" letters, which any IBMer may send to any company manager right up to chairman of the board; and by attention to IBMers' requests for open-door meetings with particular managers.

Complaints through these channels are never taken lightly —and the wise manager will not always take them literally.

Sometimes a complaint on a specific issue will be a subtle signal of trouble on a broader and deeper level of which the complainant himself may not be fully conscious. The manager may have to look for what the real trouble is.

I remember one time when I had just arrived in San Francisco for a division sales banquet and got a call from corporate headquarters. They had just received a "Speak Up" letter from one of our toolroom men in Lexington, addressed to Thomas J. Watson, Jr., at that time our board chairman. (That's how seriously we handle "Speak Ups." Minutes after the letter arrived at Armonk, New York, I was tracked down cross-country.) The complaint was as specific as could be: The toolroom was uncomfortably cold, said this man, and nobody cared enough to do anything about it. I told headquarters that indeed an unusual cold snap had hit Lexington, and that at the same time the heating system in the toolroom area had failed. It took a couple of days to fix and then was working fine.

That was a satisfactory answer, but the letter still bothered me. On my return flight from San Francisco I wondered about it. Why would a veteran toolroom man go over the heads of his department and plant managers—go to the board chairman—with a problem like that? Some deeper frustration had to be bothering him.

On my return, we sent a special interviewing team into the toolroom. Sure enough, they found a lot of dissatisfaction: People had to stand in line and go through red tape to sign out tools and supplies, machines were laid out inefficiently, lighting was unsatisfactory. People felt their managers didn't care enough to pay heed. The team probed for ideas on how the toolroom could be made more efficient—and people told them. This led to major rearrangements in the toolroom, in both physical layout and management practice, and to improved productivity. That man who lost his temper over the heating system breakdown was really saying, "This is the last straw! There's a lot wrong around here and nobody's listening. Somebody pay attention!''

A final observation on managers: Too often top managers rate their subordinates by how fast they can produce instantaneous answers to unexpected questions. That ability should be expected of computers, not managers—who should be rated on their vision and judgment, their ability to plan, and their willingness to innovate. What's wrong with a manager saying, ''I don't know. Rather than mislead you with offhand information, let me find out and give you a sure answer''? The person who says that is the one I've learned to rely on.

Perhaps even more important, when asking a manager to come up with an answer, make sure he or she knows what the question is. We were once contemplating a difficult and risky undertaking. As a precaution, one of our division executives asked an attorney to draw up a list of legal problems he foresaw if we embarked on this venture. The attorney came to a meeting the next day with a two-sheet list of possible problems. It was so scary that the people at the meeting voted to drop the venture as too impractical. Afterwards, I asked the attorney whether any of those problems was beyond reasonable solution. He said, ''Oh no. But that wasn't the question I was asked. I was just asked to list the possible problems.''

He had fulfilled his assignment. But if his assignment had been more carefully worded, we might have made an opposite —and perhaps better—decision.

16

INNOVATION
AND INNOVATORS

In a competitive system, the worst enemy of any company is the status quo. One of the most important responsibilities of top management—*the* most important responsibility in terms of company survival—is to create an atmosphere that stimulates, encourages, and rewards innovation.

Yet most top managements are devoted to the opposite—to the reduction of risk. When a new idea is presented, the instinctive response of most managers is, "How foolproof is it? What are the chances of it going wrong?" This attitude exposes them to the greatest risk of all: the risk of standing still.

Most managers will agree that innovation is important, and will say proudly, "We keep changing all the time. My company spends five percent or more of its gross income on research and development, etc., etc." That's fine, but by innovation I do not mean product development or automation or anything of a technical or physical character. What most managers resist is *management innovation*—new ways of organizing people, dealing with people, motivating people, respecting people, giving people the opportunity to convert their experience and ideas into better ways of getting a job done. One good management innovation may be more valuable—more profitable—than dozens of inventions or technical innovations.

Almost all the systems described in the preceding chapters were innovations—risky experiments—when they were undertaken. What led us to undertake them? What exempted us from the usual management tendency to resist the untried? Our Lexington management team was not gifted with genius any more than most management teams. What freed us to innovate?

Often I've thought and wondered about that, and have concluded that we were freed by previous failure. We had to innovate—or go under.

Typewriter manufacturing by IBM was put into its own plant at Lexington in the mid-1950s because for ten years the status quo hadn't worked. It didn't yield a profit. My instructions, upon taking over the function, were to innovate—to do whatever was necessary to make it profitable. The man who put me in charge added, ". . . and you report to me." Next day I asked him, "Report to you in what form?" He replied, "When you get a problem you can't solve, let me know early so that I'm not surprised if trouble should occur. Don't bother to report good news. Other than that you're on your own."

I took that literally. I rarely asked approval for anything unless it required money I didn't have at my disposal. That authority felt so good, was so liberating, that I realized others would benefit by it too. Whenever I put anyone in charge of anything, I gave him the same instructions. As I was to my superiors, my subordinates were accountable to me for results, not methods. They were not only permitted, they were *expected*, to be constantly on the lookout for new methods—and to experiment with them. We already knew the old methods weren't good enough.

For example, when I proposed to my management subordinates that we undertake the plantwide course in work simplification and they showed strong support for it, we didn't petition higher headquarters for permission. We just did it. Although the course cost hundreds of thousands of dollars in time taken from production, we felt confident the result would be a profit, not a cost. We acted on that confidence, preparing to be accountable for whatever happened.

Someone once asked me: What if a department manager had wanted to try it—wanted to shut down his line for three hours a week on the belief that he'd pick up a net gain for the effort? Should he be permitted to do it without asking permission?

Yes. He would be wise to inform his superior as to his plan, but that superior ought to have a strong reason—something better than "it's risky"—before interfering. If the innovation-minded manager turns out to be wrong, how much is really lost? If he's right, we have a transferable tool for improving productivity in every department in the plant. The odds in favor of winning—the potential gain versus the potential loss—are overwhelming.

Take the machine-floor reorganization in Lexington. It started with a request for four or five more trucks in an area already crowded with too many trucks. The spirit of innovation, instead of leading to a simple approval or disapproval, led to questions, to exploration for better ways. Management went ahead and reorganized the department—and it worked. The mini-line was a radical revision of our production methods. People believed in it, did it—and it worked. The ten-person line in Toronto was even more radical—and it worked.

The success of those ideas was almost inevitable, because they were home-grown, were carefully planned, and were the full responsibility of those who undertook them. The fact is, when people want an idea to work—even a bad idea, which none of these were—it probably will work. When people don't want an idea to work—even a good idea—it surely won't.

The most effective way to kill an innovation—worse still, to kill the spirit of innovation—is to require a round of approvals from above. Why? Because an innovation, while an opportunity for the innovator to make points and prove himself, almost always is seen as a threat by a higher manager who has to approve it—whether he's conscious of it or not. The higher manager has a built-in fear of and resistance to experimentation at lower levels. If the experiment works, the innovator will get the credit. If it fails, the person who approved it gets the blame.

So the higher-level person defends himself, in ways that appear constructive and properly cautious but are really innovation killers. He'll ask the innovator to document his argument that the innovation is likely to achieve its objective. If it's truly an innovation, how can he do that without actually trying it? More cleverly, the higher-level person may say, "Your objective is fine and the method looks good, but there may be other methods. Can you furnish two alternative methods so we can choose the best one?" Next, he'll ask why each of the alternatives shouldn't be ranked first.

All very "constructive" and cautious. But meanwhile the spirit of initiative has been knocked right out of the innovator. He wonders why he ever got into this in the first place. And what else has happened? The initiative has been stolen from the person who discovered the problem and invented a solution—the innovator—and is now in the hands of a defensive manager who is removed from the problem. If three alternative methods are proposed, the higher-level manager will judge which is best. This is like the tool-design manager who always reached for his red pencil. He needed to make the innovation *his* before okaying it. By that time, the demoralized innovator was secretly hoping the idea wouldn't work.

For these reasons, which evolve from human nature, a management that wants to encourage innovation must permit approvals on the lowest feasible managerial level—if possible, by the innovator himself. If the innovator is eager to take the risk, encourage him to take it. The possible gain probably far outweighs the possible loss.

When an innovation works, the innovator must be generously and conspicuously rewarded. The reason is obvious: to encourage other innovators and innovations. But the converse is at least equally important. If it fails, the innovator must not be penalized or castigated. He must be patted on the back for trying, and wished better luck next time. (Of course, if a person fails on two or three "bright" ideas in a row, he's not an innovator but a gambler. He may have to be encouraged to test his luck at Las Vegas on his own time and budget.)

Another ploy by innovation-resistant managers at the top is to say, "The idea may look fine in theory, but it would set a *dangerous precedent*. If it doesn't work, how could we undo it?" That is seldom valid. The experiment can be controlled by calling it just that—an experiment.

Some years ago we had the idea at Lexington that we'd like to eliminate time clocks (for reasons to be discussed in the final chapter of this book). Recognizing that this had "precedent-setting" implications, we sought and obtained corporate approval to run six departments without time clocks—as an experiment. We announced to people in those departments and throughout the plant that the experiment would be halted after 18 months, which it was. However, the information obtained from this experiment was valuable input into the corporate decision a few years later to eliminate time clocks throughout all the plants of all the divisions of IBM.

The immediate response of one of our first-line managers

was "No, it would set a dangerous precedent" when one of his assemblers, during World Series time, asked permission to play a small portable radio at his work station. That would have been the end of it, except that the assembler, to whom the decision made no sense, wrote a "Speak Up" letter of protest to the plant manager.

I happened to be at the meeting at which the letter came up. At most companies' meetings, if this issue arose the first question asked would be, "Why should we let this fellow do it? Won't everyone want to do it? Why set a dangerous precedent?" Instead, the first question at this meeting of innovation-minded managers was, "Why not?" That's usually a far more intelligent question.

Would it slow up production? No one could see how. Would it interfere with others? We decided to go back and ask the man's co-workers. None of his neighbors objected. So we established a rule permitting portable radios, provided that the entertainment did not interfere with either the owner's production or his neighbor's peace of mind.

Within a week or two, half the people in the plant had small radios at their work stations—and still do. On rare occasions, a first-line manager may have to adjudicate between the clashing musical tastes of two of his people, telling someone either to turn down his radio or to wear earphones. But such complaints are extremely rare (working neighbors do take care to be considerate of one another), and everyone appears happier for the innovative rule.

An idea that seemed like a potential problem in one plant turned out to be a clever solution in another. Our plant in Boigny, France, has an area of extremely noisy machinery which posed a threat to the ears of people working there steadily. Those people were required to wear ear plugs or ear muffs. Recently someone had the bright, innovative idea of providing ear muffs with built-in radio receivers. The walls of the area were wired with antennas emitting music on two channels. A person could choose gentle music, lively music, or silence. The innovation—a health threat converted into a pleasure—was received so well that soon people in other parts of the plant asked for the music-making ear muffs, and were given them. In either case—Lexington or Boigny—what was there to lose by trying, compared with the possible gain in personal satisfaction and morale?

Too much care in trying to avoid risk is the death knell of creativity and innovation. To use one more sports analogy, a basketball coach who wants to build a fast-breaking, aggressive team has to focus the minds of his players on points scored, not on floor errors. If his goal is a no-error game, he can probably achieve that. But the points will be racked up by the other side.

In manufacturing, top management's challenge is to provide a climate that promotes creativity and innovation, rewards success, and, above all, removes unnecessary fear of failure. Creativity is never error-free. Experimentation, by its nature, cannot always be successful. The important thing is not the few tries along the way that didn't work out, but the ones that scored big points for productivity, high morale, and further creativity.

Finally, remember that change per se—even if it is not successful—can have a rejuvenating effect on morale. Employees have a *desire* for change, not a fear of change. A plant that experiences no change gets stale, old, tiresome—boring to work in. It can be revived by a new product, a new technology, or a management innovation. The most dangerous "future shock" is the status quo.

RANDOM THOUGHTS

This final chapter is a distillation of ideas for the future that derive from 40 years of personal experience in manufacturing. That experience provided far more than just a topside view. The thoughts expressed in this chapter—and throughout this book—draw from 13 years of direct work on assembly lines and the machine floor, and from the many managerial levels in which I served, including that of plant manager, before assuming responsibility for a network of plants in the United States and abroad as division vice president for manufacturing.

The thoughts and foresights in this chapter are strictly my own. They do not represent plans of any company of which I am aware.

A NEW ERA IN THE HISTORY OF WORK

Industrialists and social observers generally sense that we are now embarking on a new stage in the long history of human work and its meaning to mankind. The previous stages of that history may be broadly divided as follows:

1. The primeval era before man invented tools.
2. The era of the wheel.and other simple tools.
3. The industrial revolution.
4. The era of scientific management.
5. The era of automation.

It is critically important, if one is to think about the future, to note the accelerating pace of change. Each of the first two eras extended for untold hundreds of generations. The third era, the industrial revolution, developed early in the nineteenth century. The fourth era, scientific management, took over at the turn of the twentieth century, followed in midcentury by the fifth, the era of automation.

As we enter the last quarter of the twentieth century, futurists are heralding still a new stage, the "post-industrial society." Unfortunately, that label gives no clue as to what they mean, and I have yet to see anyone forecast its most important human characteristics. In my view, we are moving inexorably—in fact, have already entered—into what I would call the Era of Human Concern.

As tangible symbols of the reforms ushering in this new era, a number of companies, IBM among them, have taken important steps to elevate the recognition, status, and self-esteem of people doing direct work in manufacturing. Two such steps that have particularly interested me are:

1. Placing everyone, blue collar as well as white collar people, on regular salary. This is an affirmation that those who accomplish the physical work—and thus produce the wealth—

of the company are as important a part of it as anyone else. It is a rejection of old forms of noncommitment—hourly wages and piece rates.

2. Elimination of time clocks. This step is a message to every member of a company that he is there to get a job done —and will be judged on that—rather than just to put in hours.

These were both radical innovations. Dire results were predicted by many skeptics. The problems they expected, however, never materialized. Die-hard skeptics still ask, "Where is the objective proof of change in employee attitude resulting from these steps?" There's no way to prove the case with numbers. But the message of the innovations is clear and easily recognizable to any employee: that the dignity of those who do the physical work is on the rise, that old employer attitudes are changing. That is a payoff in itself.

The job to be done is more important than the number of hours worked—and the job to be done should be the subject of management concentration. Every person, whether high on the ladder or low, whether wearing a blue collar or a white one, should have a clear and definite responsibility for a task that is equivalent to a good day's work. His chief responsibility should then be the *task*, not the *time*. With that goal in mind, almost any job can, to some degree, be unlocked from dependency on the work rate of people in other jobs. Every person then could—and should—have some discretion as to his starting time and going-home time.

One effort in this direction, now working satisfactorily in a growing number of European plants, including some in IBM, is "variable working hours," also known as "flextime." Each person (with a few exceptions, because of the special nature of certain jobs) has a discretionary period of about an hour and a half for arrival at work, and the same for leaving. By week's end each person is required to have worked his full weekly quota of hours.

Another plan would hold a person responsible for accomplishment of tasks but would not hold him accountable for hours at all. Such a plan would present a new set of management problems but would be a break away from our present system, with its misplaced emphasis on putting in time. Certainly neither of these plans is the final answer, but they show progress is being made.

"HUMAN NATURE"?

I don't believe the average employee's goal is to minimize his work or the time he spends working. He is just as concerned about inflation as any economist, and he realizes increased productivity is one way of fighting it. He would like to feel that his time is well spent and that other costs are watched carefully too.

Employees are not a company's adversaries—unless the company assumes they are, acts as if they are, and thus *makes* adversaries of its own people. People want to be helpful and loyal. But loyalty must work in two directions—downward as well as upward—or it won't work at all.

Employees have a big stake in the success of their employer —and they know it. That knowledge breeds loyalty. The way to kill that loyalty is to keep sending down the message, "While we expect you to care about us, we're too busy to care about you." On the other hand, when a company is willing to strain its reserves when necessary to demonstrate loyalty to its people, those people will readily dip into *two* reserve funds in response:

1. A reserve capability of doing more work, especially when rewarded for it, and

2. A reserve capacity for creative thought that can continually increase productivity when minds are challenged and innovators are rewarded with recognition.

PLANT DESIGN

Plants should be designed primarily not for machines, not for products, but for people.

Many companies have a rule of thumb, for example, that ceilings must be 16 feet high to accommodate machinery—even though they don't anticipate installing tall machines. Companies seldom start planning a factory by asking the question, "What ceiling height would be most elevating to the comfort of *people?*" Planners frequently ask that when starting on an office—but not a factory.

We recently broke ground for a new plant in Guadalajara, Mexico. The planning had started with that question, as well as with other "people" questions. The architect, a prize-winning designer of hotels and office buildings, was amazed—and delighted. He'd never heard of a factory planned primarily for people. When we asked if anything could be done architecturally to muffle the noise of machinery and the whirring of huge air conditioners, he replied, astonished, "But of course! No one ever asked to do it—not for a factory. But of course it can be done."

A can of cheerful orange or yellow paint costs not a penny more than a can of gloomy green or drab buff. Our Mexican plant will be colored not only for good cheer, but for a Mexican style of good cheer. Every culture has its own responses to color. The psychology of color has become a science—practiced with imagination and care for offices. Why not for factories?

In our recently completed Berlin plant, color has been used not only for cheer but for function. Each department area is decorated in a distinct color, psychologically dividing the huge manufacturing area into smaller "rooms" of green, orange, yellow, and so on. Instead of signs and pointers leading to the various departments, colored stripes along the corridors show the way. Our Berlin managers have told me (again, there's no objective way to prove this) that their colorful and cheery new plant seems to have produced a higher consciousness of personal grooming by production people who work there.

Office spaces have lately been made far more interesting through the design trend of "landscaping": dividing large office spaces into irregular-sized clusters, curving the aisles

Figure 12. Architect's conception of possible mini-line for new Guadalajara "plant for people."

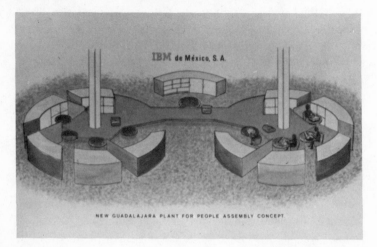

that separate them, and using color to distinguish individual areas within the large one. Why can't assembly areas be landscaped, too?

We have just such an attempt in the planning stage for our Guadalajara plant. The architect's drawing, shown in Figure 12, illustrates how personal dignity and increased comfort can harmonize with the efficiencies of a ten-person mini-line. This work area will be colorful as well—with dashes of blue, green, red, and yellow brightening up the assembly cabinets.

Is this all a costly frill? The truth is that this design may cost *less* than the conventional arrangement. Its circular motif around two supporting columns makes use of floor space which, in normal layouts, often is wasted. This may be another example of how a decision maker may use supposed extravagance as an excuse not to do something that he wasn't inclined to do in the first place.

Why has industry been so backward in making the factory a physically pleasant place to work? If industry had long ago been inclined to dignify its manual work, it long ago would have discovered that it's a low-cost, no-cost, or even profitable thing to do. A factory should be a place that every person feels proud and pleased to arrive at in the morning.

MANAGEMENT TRAINING PROGRAMS

Managers at lower levels as well as higher must be given a chance to expand educationally and to keep abreast of advances in industrial practice that may affect their work. That objective can be accomplished in three ways, not all of equal merit:

1. Company training programs.
2. Outside training programs.
3. Outside seminars on topics of industrial concern.

The first in the list, company training programs, are the most widely used, particularly for lower-level managers. They are also usually the least effective—or, at least, tend to be ranked lowest in the esteem of those who've attended all three. This is not necessarily because company programs are poor, but rather because they cannot possibly offer the advantages of the second and third methods in the list.

Being sent to an outside program is a form of special recognition. It is a tribute to a person's importance, an encouragement to an individual on the way up, a signal that the company hopes for even better things from a man or woman who has already demonstrated accomplishment. Furthermore, an outside program offers the valuable stimulation and experience of association with people from other companies. This is bound to heighten an individual's sense of professionalism in his or her work.

Another dimension of this valuable outside contact can be obtained by arranging visits by managers to plants of other companies, where they can compare notes with their peers who deal with problems that are related to but different from their own, and where they can broaden their knowledge of modern industrial practices. And, of course, the psychological lift gained by being chosen for such a visit is not to be underestimated.

RECOGNITION FOR THE PEOPLE
WHO DO THE WORK

Industry has long known the value of staging major events for the recognition of good work by nonmanagerial people such as salesmen and professional workers. Conventions and meetings for sales people are an unquestioned good investment. Engineers are accustomed to gathering at intracompany conventions and to getting together with their peers from other companies at association conventions. Other professionals attend similar meetings, with most companies gladly sending them in the interests of both education and recognition. The company that questions the value of these events is considered penny-wise, pound-foolish and far behind the times.

No company I know of, however, makes a practice—or even seriously considers the practice—of staging memorable off-site recognition events on a similar scale for people who do outstanding work in direct production. *Why not?* I have wondered why not, and only recently arrived at a simple conclusion. Meetings, conventions, even workshops, are planned to stimulate the mind. Companies have not thought in terms of stimulating the minds of those who do manual work. But as employers discover the untapped riches that lie in the minds of their personnel—who know their jobs best—they will become more eager to stimulate and expand the knowledge, enthusiasm, and opportunities of factory workers in the same degree as the aforementioned nonmanagerial groups. And I say the sooner the better.

In addition to the value of idea exchange and information distribution afforded by special meetings, one of their important functions is to raise the sense of importance of salesmen, engineers, and other groups by bringing them into closer per-

sonal contact with higher management. When the chairman
of the board thinks you and your peers are important enough
to fly cross-country to address, you can't help but be impressed
—impressed with yourself. That being so, wouldn't the same
be true many times over if factory personnel of more than
ordinary achievement were congratulated personally by the
men at the top—at a special recognition event?

And if a special recognition event provides some groups
with a valuable change of pace, a source of relaxation, a symbol of two-way loyalty, and simply something special to look
forward to, why would that value not be returned just as
handsomely by appreciative people engaged in factory work?

To translate the above observations into specific terms, I
propose that a company should annually sponsor a Manufacturing Technical Conference. I envision it as a three-day meeting located in a recognized convention city where relaxation
and enjoyment can supplement the main business of a profes-
sionally organized program of company information, technical education, and idea exchange.

Every year, 15 percent of the manufacturing personnel of
the company's plant or plants would be invited to the Manufacturing Technical Conference. They would be selected on
the following basis:

1. Ten percent through a Monthly Merit Award program—
a system for recognition of top producers, special achievers,
creators of the most valuable suggestions and innovations, etc.

2. Five percent by length of service with the company, as
a recognition of loyalty.

CHANGING DEAD-END JOBS INTO
OPEN-END JOBS

Industry and public service include a layer of so-called "low-
level" jobs, such as cleaning people, garbagemen, maids, dish-
washers, car washers, parking lot attendants, and night watch-
men. Our national employment picture could be changed and

many social problems eliminated if large-scale employers, including government, looked upon these jobs not as dead-end careers but as entrance-level jobs—tasks that people perform temporarily as a first steppingstone to more advanced responsibility earned by merit. This employer viewpoint would have to be backed by patience, modest investments in specific job training, and incentives for these employees to pick up some basic education.

If employers put out that extra effort, they will find that these less desirable jobs, often hard to fill, are suddenly more attractive to many who now shun them. Moreover, employers will find that people in such jobs will often show potential and eagerness for growth when they become convinced that promised opportunities for advancement are real. Both participants profit—employer and employee alike.

That is not idealism but is based on actual experience with a program that I helped launch in Lexington. A Lexington citizen, highly successful in several businesses, decided to start still another, as a civic-minded social experiment as well as a potential source of profit. With my encouragement—and my more tangible help in the form of modest subcontracts from our Lexington plant—he established Industrial Manpower Supply (IMS), located in an unused portion of a tobacco warehouse in the midst of the city's most impoverished neighborhood. Unemployment in that neighborhood, where both whites and blacks reside, is so prevalent that many children grow up with no clear idea of what work is. Thus what some people in the neighborhood lack, aside from the most rudimentary occupational skill, is awareness of basic work attitudes—the importance of punctuality, of showing up daily, how to talk and behave with co-workers and managers, proper grooming for the workplace, and so on.

The founder of IMS realized that these attitudes couldn't be taught in the abstract. He pledged himself to do what most employers will not do: give an individual a job *first;* prove to him or her by demonstration that good work turns into higher pay, increased trust and responsibility, and greater respect and self-respect; then patiently proceed to emphasize basic work disciplines, which by that time the individual is eager to learn. In addition to all this, IMS arranged for the Lexington public school system to assign an adult-education teacher to the project. IMS employees may attend a class for an hour a day with pay, earn school credit, and eventually qualify for a high-school equivalency certificate (which a number of IMS people have already earned).

The chief objective of IMS, which sets it apart from any profit-seeking business anyone ever heard of, is to *get rid of its best employees.* That's a fact. IMS likes to get contracts, likes to turn out good work, likes to keep its clients happy. But its main purpose is to develop a person's readiness for regular industrial employment—and seeing a client company hire that person away.

IMS started with 70 employees, all lacking experience and/ or qualifications for job openings in the city's growing community of manufacturing plants. IBM subcontracted a substantial amount of relatively simple subassembly work to IMS, involving work that we would normally assign to skill levels 12 and 13, our lowest grades, and some that we would assign to level 14. Employees were hired into the lowest skill level and advanced on merit until they reached the highest level (14). When they became highly satisfactory workers in this third level they were ready for regular employment in outside industry, and IMS found good jobs for them in other companies.

The project turned out much better than planned. The employees rapidly gained efficiency, and IMS became financially self-sustaining after a very short startup time. After a while, other neighboring companies, influenced by our satisfaction, joined us in the subcontracting experiment. To make a long and fascinating story short, within three years our plant had hired 35 people from IMS into permanent IBM jobs. Another 45 have been hired by other companies. At this writing, 75 IMS employees are at work on IBM subcontracts alone—and we hope to continue to steal some of these people away from IMS. Perhaps the most rewarding fact in this story is that many of our ex-IMS people have already earned promotions one or more times at IBM.

WOMEN—A VALUABLE RESOURCE

In a world that lately seems to be running out of everything, we hear a lot of talk about exploring, discovering, and tapping new resources. The main theme of this book has been the development of a great untapped resource—the minds of employees, particularly manual employees. My guess is that many readers will unconsciously interpret this theme as meaning the minds of men. That would be a gross misinterpretation. I mean the minds of *all* employees. If the minds of men have wastefully gone untapped, the minds of women have been wasted at least twice as much.

Examples are still far too rare of women advancing into management, or of women even being selected for training in the arts and skills of solving industrial problems. The resource of womanpower—the thinking power of women—can potentially double the problem-solving capacity of industry. On a larger scale, it can double our society's capacity to make progress in any direction it chooses to go.

Leaders in industry, the professions, and education must reexamine their prejudices, their stereotyped role-casting, and most of all their *practices* if the great untapped resource of womanpower is to be released. The job cannot be considered completed until little girls grow up with the same freedom of expectation, career ambition, and range of choice now taken for granted with regard to little boys. That will take a lot of doing—in the home, in our schools, and in industry.

IF EVERYONE USES HIS MIND,
MANAGEMENT IS STRENGTHENED

Management must manage. There is nothing "enlightened" about a management that abdicates its responsibilities in the name of "democracy" or "group participation." Dissolution of management can lead only to chaos.

That viewpoint is not at all in conflict with principles advanced throughout this book—that a person in a job knows that job best, that he or she is the person most likely to perceive new ways to make that job efficient, and that every job should be organized in such a way as to give the person doing it total responsibility for his or her work.

If those principles are implemented, the manager's position is indeed strengthened, because each of his department members, besides being a contributor of work, can be a valuable consultant to management.

A manager—on any level—who has the courage to evaluate himself in a tough-minded and realistic way ought every once in a while to lay aside his operating plans, his computer print-outs, his progress reports, all the devices that help him avoid the human issues in his department, plant, or company. He should put himself in the place of his most "average" employee, trying to sense what that person's emotions really are, and should honestly estimate how he or she would answer a certain set of questions. I, for one, have put them to myself many times, from my days as a lowly beginner and on through the years:

"Driving by the plant on a Sunday, do I feel a warm glow? Do I point it out with pride to my children? Or do I get a sinking feeling at the thought of having to go back in there tomorrow?"

In my working life, I have known both feelings.

INDEX